Hg2 Stockholm

A Hedonist's guide to
Stockholm

BY Scarlett Stapleton
PHOTOGRAPHY Scarlett Stapleton

A Hedonist's guide to Stockholm

Managing director – Tremayne Carew Pole
Series editor – Catherine Blake
Production – Navigator Guides
Design – P&M Design
Typesetting – Dorchester Typesetting
Repro – PDQ Digital Media Solutions Ltd
Printer – Printed in Italy by Printer Trento srl
PR – Ann Scott Associates
Publisher – Filmer Ltd
Additional photography - Tremayne Carew Pole

Email – info@ahedonistsguideto.com
Website – www.ahedonistsguideto.com

First published in the United Kingdom in 2004 by
Filmer Ltd
47 Filmer Road
London SW6 7JJ

ISBN – 0-9547878-2-X

Hg2 Stockholm

CONTENTS

How to...

A Hedonist's guide to... is broken down into easy to use sections:
Sleep, Eat, Drink, Snack, Party, Culture, Shop, Play and Info. In each of
these sections you will find detailed reviews and photographs.

At the front of the book you will find an introduction to the city and
an overview map, followed by descriptions to the four main areas and
more detailed maps. On each of these maps you will see the places
that we have reviewed, laid out by section, highlighted on the map with
a symbol and a number. To find out about a particular place, simply
turn to the relevant section, where all entries are listed alphabetically.

Alternatively, browse through a specific section (i.e. Eat) until you find
a restaurant that you like the look of. Next to your choice will be a
small coloured dot – each colour refers to a particular area of the city
– then simply turn to the relevant map to discover the location.

Updates

Due to the lengthy publishing process and shelf lives of books it is
very difficult to keep travel guides up to date – new restaurants, bars
and hotels open up all the time, while others simply fade away or just
go out of style. What we can offer you are free updates – simply log
onto our website www.ahedonistsguideto.com or www.hg2.net and
enter your details, answer a relevant question to provide proof of pur-
chase and you will be entitled to free updates for a year from the date
that you sign up. This will enable you to have all the relevant information at your finger tips whenever you go away.

In order to help us, if you have any comments or recommendations
that you would like to see in the guide in future please feel free to
email us at info@ahedonistsguideto.com.

The concept

A Hedonist's guide to… is designed to appeal to a more urbane and stylish traveller. The kind of traveller who is interested in gourmet food, elegant hotels and seriously chic bars – the traveller who feels the need to explore, shop and pamper themselves away from the madding crowd.

Our aim is to give you the inside knowledge of the city, to make you feel like a well-heeled, sophisticated local and to take you to the most fashionable places in town to rub shoulders with the local glitterati.

In today's world work rules our life, weekends away are few and far between, and when we do go away we want to have the most fun and relaxation possible with the minimum of stress. This guide is all about maximizing time. Everywhere is photographed, so before you go you know exactly what you are getting into; choose a restaurant or bar that suits you and your demands.

We pride ourselves on our independence and our integrity. We eat in all the restaurants, drink in all the bars and go wild in the nightclubs – all totally incognito. We charge no one for the privilege of appearing in the guide; every place is reviewed and included at our discretion.

We feel cities are best enjoyed by soaking up the atmosphere and the vibrancy; wander the streets, indulge in some retail relaxation therapy, re-energize yourself with a massage and then get ready to eat like a king and party hard on the stylish local scene.

We feel that it is important for you to explore a city on your own terms, while the places reviewed provide definitive coverage in our eyes; one's individuality can never be wholly accounted for. Sometimes if you take that little extra time to wander off our path, then you may just find that truly hidden gem that we missed.

Stockholm

Is Stockholm a city for winter or summer visits? The answer is that it's perfect for hedonists at any time of year. Lounge outside in summer in one of the picturesque squares; or relax blissfully by the fire in a warm bar or restaurant in the winter. It's small by capital-city standards; so small, in fact, that it is possible to see most of the sights in a couple of days without excessive effort. The essential cultural edifices can be visited easily in a few hours with a prolonged intermission for a luxurious lunch. Save some time for an expedition to the archipelago, whether by boat in summer or on skates in winter, and a wander round the city's most famous museum, the Vasamuseet, but otherwise just allow yourself to be seduced by this beautiful, relaxed and stylish gem.

The best way to get around is on foot; distances are invariably short and you may find less well-known treasures *en route*. So, girls, take your trainers! If your Blahniks and Choos are irreplaceable and therefore *à pied* is not your preferred mode of transport, or you just don't believe in taking exercise, the tube system is amazingly simple. However, the real hedonist will only take taxis; fares can be extortionate, but on the bright side they do take credit cards. They come in handy for the really worthwhile trips, such as the 20-minute ride out of the city to the Michelin-starred restaurant Edebacka Krog, or a day trip to the Yasuragi spa.

There's a fantastic selection of top restaurants in Stockholm, and you'll be spoilt for choice. The city rejoices in an incredible diversity of cuisines of an exceptionally high standard. There are quite a number of Michelin-starred spots; mouth-watering food and feel-good ambience are abundant from the business-orientated Fredsgatan 12 to the opulent Operakallaren.

The high standards are maintained in the bars and clubs – most restaurants double as bars so their opening hours are long and late throughout the week. Legally Stockholm bars are not allowed to serve alcohol without offering at the least a snack, so you can eat pretty well, even if your intention was only to have a quick drink at the end of a day working, walking or sightseeing.

The words that most appropriately describe Stockholm's atmosphere, architecture and party culture are those that successfully sum up the city's inhabitants: young, attractive, vibrant and elegant. Stockholm and its natives fill you with the overwhelming sense that this small, bustling metropolis is indeed the foremost up-and-coming place to drink, eat and party in Europe. While the city has never been unpopular, a surge in glacially 'cool' designers and the major players in the IT and mobile phone business have caused the upturn in fortunes. This has allowed a thriving restaurant and bar scene to emerge, populated by the glamorous and chic acolytes of the new millennium. Stockholm is cool, Stockholm can afford to be expensive.

Since the city is built on a raft of different islands it is easily divided into navigable areas. To help you plan your itinerary, we've concentrated on the four districts that will prove most useful for a hedonist in Stockholm: Gamla Stan, Östermalm, Norrmalm/Vasastan and Södermalm.

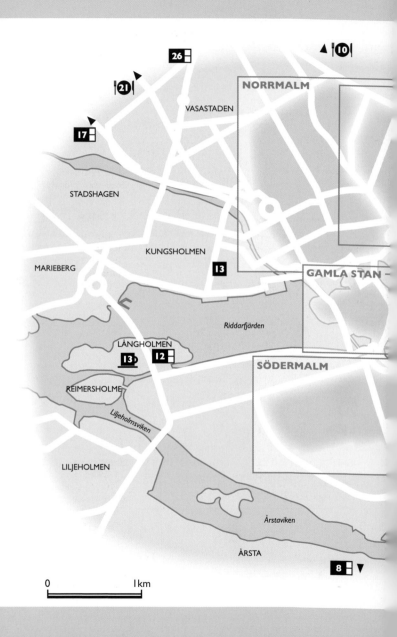

NORRMALM

GAMLA STAN

SÖDERMALM

VASASTADEN

STADSHAGEN

KUNGSHOLMEN

MARIEBERG

Riddarfjärden

LÅNGHOLMEN

REIMERSHOLME

Liljeholmsviken

LILJEHOLMEN

Årstaviken

ÅRSTA

26

21

17

13

13

12

8

10

0   1 km

Stockholm city map

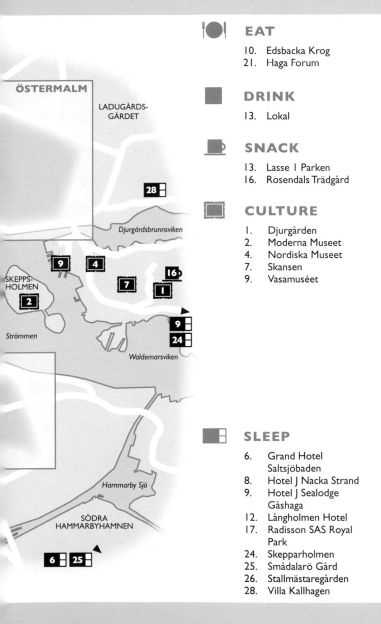

ÖSTERMALM

LADUGÅRDS-
GÄRDET

Djurgårdsbrunnsviken

SKEPPS-
HOLMEN

Strömmen

Waldemarsviken

Hammarby Sjö

SÖDRA
HAMMARBYHAMNEN

EAT

10. Edsbacka Krog
21. Haga Forum

DRINK

13. Lokal

SNACK

13. Lasse I Parken
16. Rosendals Trädgård

CULTURE

1. Djurgården
2. Moderna Museet
4. Nordiska Museet
7. Skansen
9. Vasamuséet

SLEEP

6. Grand Hotel
   Saltsjöbaden
8. Hotel J Nacka Strand
9. Hotel J Sealodge
   Gåshaga
12. Långholmen Hotel
17. Radisson SAS Royal
   Park
24. Skepparholmen
25. Smådalarö Gård
26. Stallmästaregården
28. Villa Kallhagen

Gamla Stan

There is an equivalent of Gamla Stan in every city – the place that is supposedly packed full of character and, as a result, is packed full of tourists. The Old Town in Stockholm is no exception to this rule. Cobbled streets and rustic-looking shops sell every possible souvenir to bring in the guided tours. Despite this, however, it remains simply irresistible.

Lose yourself in the maze of little terracotta-coloured buildings, most of which look as if they're about to fall apart. Shops and restaurants have cashed in on its appeal and have created an artificial charm, yet part of the authentic Stockholm undoubtedly survives, and a night in a hotel on one of the winding streets is undoubtedly a pleasure.

Your choice of hotel is basically limited to the Bengsston trio – The Victory, the Lord Nelson and the Lady Hamilton, all of which have retained a traditional feel and illustrate different aspects of Scandinavian life. The Victory especially is a great fusion of the old-fashioned and the luxurious.

Aside from the mass of red-chequered tables in every other bistro, there are a couple of exquisite restaurants that have managed to avoid too much kitsch. Top of the list are the renowned Pontus in the Greenhouse and the two Ruby restaurants which, unusually for the area, are more popular with Stockholm's locals than tourists.

Looming over the Old Town is the Kungliga Slottet, the Royal Palace. Less beautiful than striking, it is the official residence of the royal family. The palace is open to the public and the tours around the Royal Apartments provide a unique insight into the lives of a very down-to-earth royal family. The waterfront, while not as beautiful as Östermalm's Strand, affords you a memorable view of the picturesque island of Skeppsholmen.

Gamla Stan is a treasure. Soak up the atmosphere, try to ignore the backpackers and find an inconspicuous café for a hot chocolate on a cold afternoon while you decide where to go next. Right in the centre of Stockholm, Gamla Stan provides access to all the other major islands; in summer, board the ferry across to Djurgården to take in the sights.

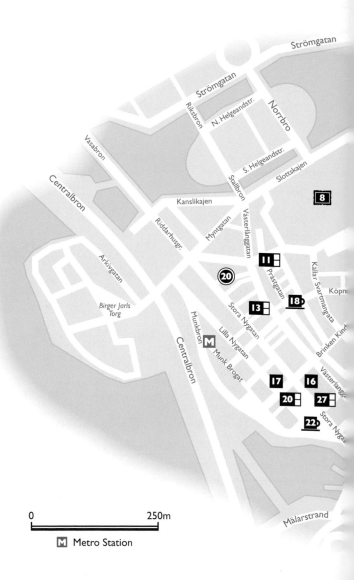

0   250m

M Metro Station

Gamla Stan local map

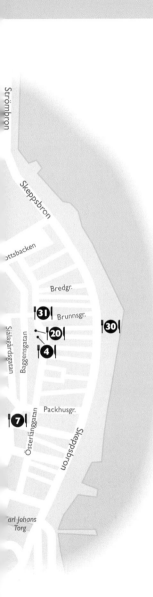

DRINK

16. Markattan
17. Mistral

SNACK

18. St Göran & Draken
22. Tabac

CULTURE

8. Royal Palace

SLEEP

11. Lady Hamilton Hotel
13. Lord Nelson
20. Rica City Hotel
27. The Victory

PARTY

20. Stampen

EAT

4. Bistro Ruby
7. Den Gyldene Freden
20. Grill Ruby
30. Pontus' Brasserie by the Sea
31. Pontus in the Greenhouse

Östermalm

Chic, chic, chic. Östermalm is the haunt of Stockholm's elite. Elegant and beautiful, its inhabitants mirror the architecture, shopping and restaurant scene. In the exclusive bars and restaurants models, pop-stars, international playboys and actors party hand-in-hand with royalty.

Situated to the north of Gamla Stan, it provides the necessary antidote to the narrow cobbled streets and the 'authentic' souvenir shops of the Old Town. The long and open boulevard that is Birger Jarlsgatan is home to some of Stockholm's finest shops and designer outlets, and in summer the large open squares such as Stureplan and Östermalmstorg provide seating areas for the cafés and bars where the young and the beautiful gather.

Everything about Östermalm is up-market: from its shops to its bars, the district hums with the chatter of what's hot and what's not; new venues open up every day and the old successfully trundle on thanks largely to their location. Some of the hippest and most difficult places to get into are found in this part of town, close to Stureplan: Kharma, Berns and the Lydmar are legendary local establishments that demand and receive only the finest of Stockholm's socialites.

Despite such a wealth of nightlife and gourmet experiences, this district is still largely residential. Property here is understandably expensive; its neo-classical architecture is typified by opulent hotels such as the Grand and the Diplomat, whose façades overlook the waterfront. Fashionable living is the key, and if you've come to Stockholm for nothing more than stunning architectural triumphs and a decadent night out, you may find yourself reluctant to venture to other districts.

If you decide to stay in Östermalm, then there are some staggeringly beautiful and well-designed hotels: the Grand, Berns and Diplomat to name a few. Here the order of the day is total hedonism. You will be treated like visiting royalty in wonderful surroundings. It is more expensive than elsewhere in town, but it does put you right at the centre of the action.

While not overly imbued with culture, Östermalm is home to the National Museum and the Museum of Modern Art – these two galleries take in the spectrum of Swedish art and design from the 16th century to the present day. Just over the water is the amazing Djurgården, where the Skansen, Nordic and the Vasa museums are found, along with beautiful parkland to help you walk off those delicious meals. Alternatively pop into Saluhallen and let the range of fresh produce assail your senses and tempt you to a long and luxurious lunch.

0   250m

M Metro Station

Karlavägen

Sturegatan

Engelbrektsgatan

23

10

M

25

5   **10**

14

Linnégatan

14   **8**

23

3   **3**

Grev Tureg.

10   **16**   **16**   M   **14**   **3**

11

17

Stureplan

9   **11**   **5**   **25**   **41**

Kungsg.

7   **14**   **23**   **8**

19   **10**   **15**

Birger Jarlsgatan

9   **11**   **11**   **2**

6   **5**

Biblioteksg.

12   **9**

20   **10**   **1**

3   **29**   **1**

Riddargatan

4

20   **36**

34

Hamngatan   **17**

4

4   **21**

M

Stallg.

● PARTY

5. Cocktail Club
7. Elverket
8. Kharma
9. Koket
10. The Lab
11. Laroy
14. O Baren
16. Spy Bar
17. Sture Compagniet

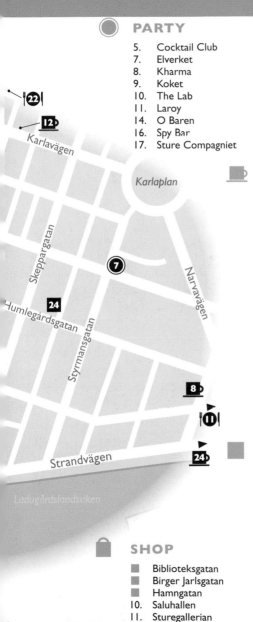

■ SNACK

2. Baresso
3. Bonan
4. Café Albert
8. Coco & Carmen
9. Crème
11. Elt Litet Hak
12. Foam
14. Lisa Pä Torget
15. Petite
17. Soap Bar
19. Sturehof
20. Sturekattan
21. T-Bar
23. Tures
24. Tvillingarnas

■ DRINK

1. Anna Khan
3. Aubergine
5. Brasserie Godot
6. Buddha Bar
7. East
8. Grodan
9. Halv Trappa Plus Gard
10. Hotellet
12. Isole
14. Lydmar
20. Soap Bar
24. Tudor Arms
25. Undici

■ SHOP

■ Biblioteksgatan
■ Birger Jarlsgatan
■ Hamngatan
10. Saluhallen
11. Sturegallerian

Norrmalm/Vasastan

Officially named Vasastaden, this district is most commonly known as Vasastan. The boundaries between this area, Östermalm and the city district of Norrmalm are difficult to define. Stockholm inhabitants refer more to the former two categories, but it is useful to be aware of the business quarter that nestles in between them. From the hustle and bustle of the Norrmalm/Vasastan streets, the rest of Stockholm is at your fingertips.

Vasastan/Norrmalm is home to some fabulous shopping. There are the department stores of PUB, PK Huset and NK which between them sell virtually anything that you'll ever need. Then there is Hötorget, outside the Concert Hall, which specializes in fresh flowers and vegetables during the week and becomes a flea market on a Sunday. Alternatively just wander the streets of Drottninggatan and Hamngatan browsing more familiar high street shops.

At night the area buzzes with frenetic activity and the streets are lit with the neon light emanating from cinemas and bars. However it is less exclusive and fashionable than Östermalm. During the week the

clientele tend to consist mainly of local bankers and financiers and at weekends the locals and less fashion conscious Stockholmers come out to play.

This commercial feel of Norrmalm accounts for one side of the district, while the other, Vasastan is more residential. Here the buzz is less immediately apparent. This shouldn't put party-goers off, since gems like Storstad and Olssons Skor have given these streets renewed life

and spirit. Thanks to these establishments Vasastan is becoming increasingly hip; those bored with Östermalm's over-familiarity flock here in search of a more interesting vibe.

Norrmalm is home to the über-stylish Nordic Light hotel, whose ingenious interplays of light create one of the best designed hotels in Stockholm. Many of the places to stay here are, as you might expect, business orientated. This does not necessarily go hand in hand with sterility but they do tend to be less design conscious.

This is Stockholm at its most practical – sensible shops, functional hotels, reasonably priced restaurants and decent bars. There are always exceptions to this rule but Norrmalm/Vasastan does not have the flair of Östermalm, the bohemian spirit of Södermalm or the charm of Gamla Stan.

Norrtullsgatan

Karlsbergsvägen

Dalagatan

Västmannag.

Norrmalm/Vasastan   local map

0   250   500m

Ⓜ Metro Station

Södermalm

Vasastan might be up-and-coming, but Södermalm is the place to be for a really alternative atmosphere. This is Stockholm with attitude. Relax here in the knowledge that you're not being observed or judged on what you wear or where you drink; here, the focus is on being out-of-the-ordinary. The importance of individuality confronts you on every street corner. It's evident in everything from what people wear to the free-spirited mood of juice bars, yoga studios and second-hand clothes stores. Brightly coloured clothes light up shop windows, and dread-locked salespeople chat to scruffy regulars. If you're looking for a Starbucks or a Gap, think again, turn around and head for Vasastan or Norrmalm.

As for places to go, you really have to seek them out, and when you do stumble across something it will tend to be edgier and more underground than the design-led fashion statements in Östermalm.

Södermalm has some fantastic, secluded little places to eat in. Lo Scudetto is totally unpretentious and provides excellent Italian food in cosy surroundings; alternatively, Folkhemmet or Stjernan foster a

trendy scene spiced up with fantastic food. South Stockholm also offers up the crazy fun of Koh Phangan beloved by the dope-smoking crowd. Drugs are by no means a big feature in Stockholm, but here more than anywhere the bohemian atmosphere may give rise to an odd whiff of hash.

Shops, bars and restaurants are, despite their more decrepit surroundings, not much less expensive than those of wealthy areas; certainly you will be enjoying drinks for approximately the same prices. However, each establishment is unique and strives to stand out from the crowd, differentiating itself through imaginative decor and an original breed of clientele.

Stockholm is not famous for its red-light district, mainly because it doesn't have one, but anything resembling this is found in Södermalm. Although there are some harmless and amusing shops selling racy lingerie, a few of the streets here nevertheless have a slightly seedier atmosphere. However, like the rest of Stockholm, it is safe and the chances of getting mugged remain slow.

PARTY

13. Metró
19. Mosebacke

SLEEP

3. Clarion
7. Hilton Slussen
22. Rival AB

EAT

12. Folkhemmet
15. Frya Knop
18. Gondolen
24. Koh Phangan
26. Lo Scudetto
35. Stiernan

DRINK

2. Anno 1647

SNACK

1. 7 Knop
26. Zucchero

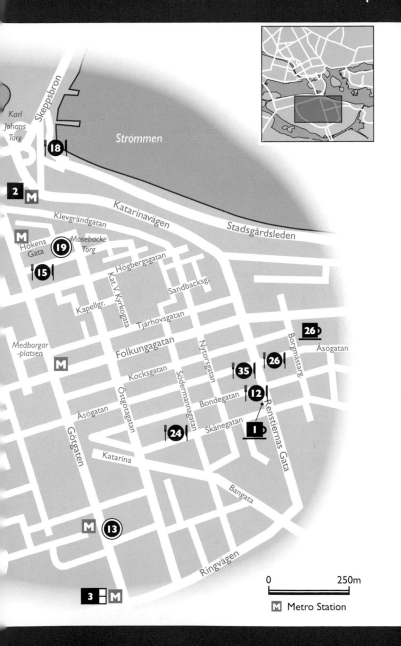

Karl Johans Torg

Skeppsbron

Strömmen

18

2

M

Katarinavägen

Klevgrändgatan

Stadsgårdsleden

M

Hökens Gata

19

Mosebacke Torg

15

Högbergsgatan

Sandbacksg.

Kat. V. Kyrkogata

Kapellgr.

Tjärhovsgatan

26

Medborgar-platsen

M

Folkungagatan

Nytorgsgatan

Borgmästarg.

Åsögatan

35

26

Kocksgatan

Östgötagatan

Södermannagatan

Bondegatan

12

Åsögatan

24

Skånegatan

1

Renstiernas Gata

Götgatan

Katarina

Bangata

M

13

Ringvägen

3

M

0   250m

M Metro Station

sleep...

Stockholm is essentially a small city and there are consequently fewer really high-class hotels than in Paris or New York. However, the presence of the more design-minded international chains, as well as some unique independent hotels, means that it is not hard to find a first-class place to stay.

Along with favourites such as the Grand, or much-loved business hotels like the Radisson Strand, there are less conspicuous treasures that offer highly original touches. Among these is the über-modern Berns, with its high-tech facilities and Bang & Olufsen systems installed, it seems, in every available space. And then there's the newly opened Rival, which, in terms of original décor and dedication to its guests' every possible need, is in a class of its own. A 'pillow menu' in each room speaks for the hotel's standards of luxury.

If you're none too keen on the popular minimalist trends of the moment, the Bengtsson hotels of Gamla Stan present old-fashioned charm. This is not to say that they are any less luxurious; along with its tastefully furnished standard rooms, The Victory offers a suite to die for. The Lord Nelson and Lady Hamilton are less grand, but have a traditional appeal and high levels of comfort.

Stockholm's tourist board as yet does not offer a graded star system, and therefore hotels work hard to promote their attractions and are aware of the need to update their facilities continually to compete. All the hotels in this section are of a very high standard, whether they're conventional, contemporary or more unusual in style. Stockholm's hotels cater for a wide range of needs and tastes, and those that do not have plasma screens or state-of-the-art hi-fis make up for it in other ways.

The glorious thing about this city is that within 15 minutes of the centre you are immersed in the loveliness of the countryside, with its beautiful views over lakes and rivers, and gardens that stretch as far as the eye can see. This means, of course, that if you'd rather not be in the centre of the action or within easy reach of a party, you can choose a country hotel yet still be close to all the city has to offer. If this idea appeals to you, check out the Villa Källhagen and the two J brand hotels.

Despite the lack of grading system, hotels can be categorized by rates, even though the variation is not all that great. Most decent hotels are expensive, but there are ways of getting round this. The majority of hotels offer good deals at certain times of year and, if you do your research, you could end up in one of the best in town at an extremely reasonable rate.

It is crucial to remember the weekday/weekend system. Hotels here keep their rates high during the week since this is when their clientele consists largely of businessfolk. Unusually, therefore, weekend rates are much lower, sometimes by almost 50%. This can obviously make a big difference to your stay in Stockholm, reducing overall expenditure considerably or just giving you more to spend on pure indulgence.

The rates given are based on the rack-rate double in low season and stretch to a suite in peak season. Each hotel is assessed according to style, atmosphere and location, to give you an idea of whether the hotel is right for you.

Our top ten hotels in Stockholm are:
1. Grand Hotel, Östermalm
2. Berns
3. Villa Källhagen
4. The Victory
5. Stallmästaregården
6. Hotel J Sealodge Gåshaga
7. Lydmar Hotel
8. Radisson SAS Strand
9. Rival AB
10. Smådalarö Gård

Our top five hotels for style are:
1. Rival AB
2. Grand Hotel, Östermalm
3. Berns
4. Stallmästaregården
5. Nordic Light

Our top five hotels for atmosphere are:
1. Berns
2. Grand Hotel, Östermalm
3. The Victory
4. Hotel J Sealodge Gåshaga
5. Villa Källhagen

Our top five hotels for location are:
1. Berns
2. Grand Hotel, Östermalm
3. Villa Källhagen
4. Lydmar Hotel
5. Radisson SAS Strand

Berns, Näckströmsgatan 8, Norrmalm.
Tel: 566 322 00 www.berns.se
Rates: 1,235–6,305kr

Where the Grand exudes old Hollywood glamour, Berns, its
sister hotel, is more about style. Gone are the chandeliers and
the plush red velvet, replaced by a more functional look. The
rooms, equipped with every conceivable mod-con, are furnished

in masculine colours and unembellished wood. This is 'bling bling'
with creature comforts: TVs appear from nowhere and top-of-
the range stereo systems ensure that MTV is accessible whether
you're lying in bed or in the bath. Extravagant and
elegant dark colours give rooms a clean finish, and everything is
tidy – a rotating cylindrical console houses the TV, minibar and
CD player. With all this, plus excellent service, the 65 rooms are
filled with a mix of successful businessmen and pop-stars seeking
refuge in a hotel slightly more discreet than the Grand. As you
might expect, rates can be higher than average, although good
deals are available off-season. Situated close to the waterfront
and in the same complex as an über-chic restaurant, bar and
nightclub, this is the Metropolitan Hotel of Stockholm.

Style 9, Atmosphere 8, Location 9

Birger Jarl, Tulegatan 8, Norrmalm.
Tel: 674 18 00 www.birgerjarl.se
Rates: 1,170–4,420kr

Despite its great location, at first sight the Birger Jarl seems rather bland, housed in an uninteresting 1970s building. However, what makes the Birger Jarl special are the 12 individually styled rooms, created by different Swedish designers and based on Nordic seasons, colour and light. Predominantly green rooms decorated with photos of pine forests and light-projected firs on the walls contrast with Spartan all-white suites with sumptuous rugs and enormous plasma TVs. The remaining standard rooms are typically Scandinavian with simple furniture and white walls. An additional attraction is the relaxation room downstairs, which plays with changing light. Situated in a smart part of town, Birger Jarl is surrounded by restaurants and bars, so you'll soon find yourself immersed in Stockholm's vibrant nightlife.

Style 8, Atmosphere 7, Location 6

Clarion Hotel, Ringvägen 98, Södermalm.
Tel: 462 10 00 www.clarionstockholm.com
Rates: 1,690–3,445kr

Another of Stockholm's recently opened hotels, the Clarion seems not to suffer from a name that doesn't altogether inspire confidence. The reason for this is immediately clear as you walk through the entrance, as the hotel has gone overboard in its efforts to be innovative and different. Retro 70s furniture litters the lobby, with the theme continuing through to the bar, restaurants and conference centre. Much of the décor works well and the odd misplaced neon sofa is not a serious enough eyesore to detract from the hotel's other qualities. The most noticeable feature is space; huge unfilled areas and high ceilings make the

public rooms, and the lobby especially, seem never-ending. The bedrooms are less over-the-top and very comfortable. Here white is the predominant colour, its starkness eased by fluffy duvets and brightly coloured cushions haphazardly strewn around. A fitness centre is luxurious enough to command an hour or so of your time, and only slightly spoilt by its view over a motorway (triple-glazed windows prevent the intrusion of any noise). Its location is not the best but, since Stockholm is so small, this shouldn't impede your exploration of the city.

Style 8, Atmosphere 7, Location 5

Diplomat, Strandvägen 7c, Östermalm.
Tel: 459 68 00 www.diplomathotel.com
Rates: 1,560–5,785kr

Close to the main theatre, Diplomat attracts a creative clientele in search of traditional comfort. Developed as a hotel in 1966 from an embassy built in 1911, it still retains many of its original features, such as stained-glass windows and an old-fashioned cocktail bar. Newly renovated, the hotel now combines the classic with the modern, and rooms are luxuriously furnished with huge beds and richly coloured fabrics. The hotel's Strand location is a huge advantage, as most of the rooms have fantastic views over the water, and the best bars, restaurants and clubs in town are close by. This is particularly relevant as Diplomat only has one bar/café. T Bar (see page 144) is excellent for a quick cocktail or superb English afternoon tea, but you'll have to head out to one of the many nearby establishments to find a three-course meal. Unusually for a hotel of this calibre, there is no spa or fitness centre, but this is in keeping with its traditional style. Its lack of ultra-modern features found in such hotels as Berns is more than made up for by location and overall lavish comfort.

Style 7, Atmosphere 7, Location 8

Grand Hôtel, S Blasieholmshammen 8, Östermalm.
Tel: 679 35 00 www.grandhotel.se
Rates: 1,560–13,000kr

This is where anyone who is anyone will beg, borrow or steal to get a room. Despite challenges from the more chic hotels such as Berns and the Lydmar the Grand has still retained its status as Stockholm's number one. Location and service are without equal, while the old-world glamour of red plush furnishings, gilded furniture and grand chandeliers adorn some of the largest and grandest suites in town. Its position on the waterfront affords breathtakingly beautiful views, especially from the terrace. Opened in 1874, the hotel has retained many of its original features and its neo-classical façade is one of the many city landmarks. While newer, design-led hotels impress with their facilities, the Grand inspires through sheer decadence. Bankers, tourists and the cognoscenti are drawn to its award-winning luxury and seamless style.

Style 9, Atmosphere 9, Location 9

Grand Hotel, Saltsjöbaden, Hotellvagen 1, 13383 Saltsjöbaden.
Tel: 506 170 25 www.grandsaltsjobaden.se
Rates: 1,300–1,690kr

Not to be confused with the Grand in the city centre, this hotel lies just outside central Stockholm. Although you feel as if you are in the heart of the countryside, in fact you are close enough to venture into town for dinner. The lobby overlooks sailing boats moored in the harbour, and you will be breathing in fresh sea air from the moment you arrive. The rooms are spacious and cheerfully decorated with citrus colours, creating a bright and breezy mood. This extends to the very superior restaurant, called Franska Matsalen just like the restaurant of its namesake hotel. In contrast to the rich, dark colours of the dining room in the Stockholm Grand, Saltsjöbaden's interior has a lighter opulence, and yellow predominates. The hotel is most suitable for summer visits when the delights of the sea can be fully appreciated, but on a rainy day there's always the impressive billiard room to keep you entertained if you don't fancy a ride into town.

Style 7, Atmosphere 7, Location 8

Hilton Slussen, Guldgränd, Box 15270, Slussen.
Tel: 517 353 00 www.hilton.com
Rates: 1,690–3,900kr

Although Hilton hotels have a good reputation for comfort and attentive service, one no longer expects them to be the sumptuous masterpieces they once were. The Hilton Slussen, however, has tried to break away from the ubiquitous business-traveller look and attempted something different. Since it's set high up on the river bank, the views over Riddarfjarden towards Gamla Stan from the restaurant, and some of the suites are delightful. The hotel has been recently redesigned to make the most of the original art deco motifs: long architectural curves pervade throughout, and are brought together to create immediately recognizable patterns. In addition, the distinctive use of light and dark striped wood in the corridors and bedrooms and stylish marble bathrooms gives a very mainstream hotel an individual touch. Of course the Hilton is equipped with every mod-con,

including a state-of-the-art gym and decent restaurant. Its location in the more bohemian Södermalm is not entirely in keeping with the more conventional type of traveller and businessman that the hotel generally attracts.

Style 6, Atmosphere 7, Location 7

**Hotel J Nacka Strand, Ellensviksvägen 1,
131 27 Nacka Strand.**
Tel: 601 30 00 www.hotelj.se
Rates: 1,040–3,185kr

With enough boutique hotels in Stockholm to satisfy a wide range of personalities, pinpointing one that outdoes the rest is something of a gamble. That said, the first of the two J hotels must come pretty close to perfection in most people's eyes. Offering something for everyone, it combines waterfront tranquillity, slightly distanced from but still within easy reach of the city hubbub, with nautical cool and first-class service. It's airy and flooded with light, and its colour-scheme is reminiscent of a sailing club – white and blue coverings swathe deep sofas and introduce the marine theme to the bedrooms. This outdoors atmosphere is offset by blazing fires in the breakfast/tea lounge, where croissants and cakes are available most of the day. Although its warmth is tremendously comforting in the winter months, staying here in August is an equally pleasant experience. You can fill carefree summer days walking in the countryside, lounging in a deckchair on the veranda, or taking the short boat ride across to Stockholm's sights. During the week J is inundated with businessmen seeking relief from days of city meetings, but at weekends, when Stockholm's residents escape the party life for a few days of calm, you can expect a more local feel.

Style 8, Atmosphere 8, Location 8

Hotel J Sealodge Gåshaga, Värdshusvägen 14–16, 181 63 Lidingö.
Tel: 601 34 10 www.hotelj.se
Rates: 1,040–2,990kr

Of the two J brand hotels (see above), the Sealodge is the less talked about, but it's just as luxurious and deserves similar rave reviews. It's situated further out of the city, but the hour's boat ride through the archipelago to Lidingö Island is a pleasure, and it's only 15 minutes to Stureplan by car, so convenient if you are in a hurry. The benefit of this hotel, however, is partly its isolation. With views over the sea stretching for miles, enjoy the fresh

air and solitude from the comfort of deckchairs on your balcony. Inside, rooms are kitted out with deep armchairs and thick blankets in nautical colours. Simple luxury is what it is all about – clean living with all the creature comforts. The immaculate style also extends to the restaurant: the fact that people travel from central Stockholm just to lunch here bears testimony to its excellence. Whether you're basking outside in the sunshine or warming your hands by a roaring fire in the chill of winter, you'll find the unpretentious luxury offered by both hotel and restaurant enormously comforting.

Style 8, Atmosphere 8, Location 9

Hotel Riddargatan, Riddargatan 14, Östermalm.
Tel: 555 730 00 www.hotelriddargatan.se
Rates: 1,040–3,900kr

This hotel is all about location: although very comfortable, it has nothing unusual to offer. Nevertheless, as an independent hotel, it has become incredibly popular during its two-year existence, possibly for its understated but tasteful décor, friendly staff and quiet position. The lack of restaurant is almost a blessing: if it had one, you would not be forced to seek out nearby spots, many of which – Anna Khan, Riche and PA and Co. included – epitomize modern Stockholm life. There is, however, a cheerfully red-lit bar in the centre of what is, from 7 to 11am, the breakfast room.

Unlikely as this may seem, the daily transition from cereals, croissants and the morning paper to martinis and pre-dinner chat is
smooth. This is because of the adaptable furnishings and cream
walls spotted with high-fashion photographs of international
stars. The rooms have an air of modernity and quiet exclusivity,
while not going overboard on the trend-setting concepts so
popular in better-known places. Primarily a Scandinavian idea, the
classic white and blue décor is ever-present, although each room
manages to assume its own unique identity.

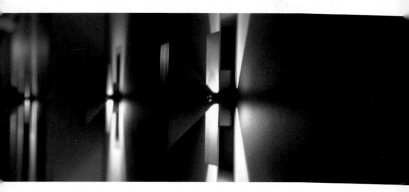

Style 7, Atmosphere 6, Location 9

Lady Hamilton Hotel, Storkyrkobrinken 5, Gamla Stan.
Tel: 506 401 00 www.lady-hamilton.se
Rates: 1,040–3,055kr

One of three hotels under the same ownership, the Lady
Hamilton is a more refined version of The Victory. Here, history
and botany replace The Victory's nautical theme, with the rooms
named after different wild flowers, and decorated with folk art
and dried flowers. The hotel oozes traditional charm: there
seems to be a preponderance of prettily painted chests and
grandfather clocks, and the bedrooms are crammed with interesting trinkets and knick-knacks. It was converted from a private
house in 1975, and has not lost that feeling of nurturing family

warmth. It is immediately apparent that a lot of effort has gone into the creation and decoration of such a comfortable environment. There are plenty of mod-cons, and a sauna and plunge pool in the basement top off the traditional Swedish touch. This is Gamla Stan appeal with a touch of extravagance.

Style 8, Atmosphere 8, Location 8

Långholmen Hotel, Långholmsmuren 20, Långholmen
Tel: 720 85 00 www.langholmen.com
Rates: 715–1,430kr

This must be Stockholm's most unusual hotel. Långholmen is a converted jail and has styled itself on the fact. You sleep in what was once a cell, with iron bars across the window and beds chained to the wall. Depressing, you might say, but the hotel is airy and entertaining and for novelty factor alone is worth at least a brief visit. The gardens are also a treat: on a sunny day Långholmen takes on all the qualities of the countryside. If prison life has taken its toll and you don't fancy staying here for meals, remember that you're only minutes by taxi from Stockholm central. Rooms are very reasonably priced, and with part of the hotel functioning as a youth hostel, tourists are in abundance. This should not put you off, as there is enough space for you to avoid too much contact with fellow holiday-makers.

> **Style 8, Atmosphere 7, Location 7**

Lord Nelson Hotel, Västerlånggatan 22, Gamla Stan.
Tel: 506 401 20 www.lady-hamilton.se
Rates: 845–2,210kr

The least fancy of the Bengtsson family hotels, the Lord Nelson doesn't live up to the Lady Hamilton or The Victory. Nestling between souvenir shops on a tourist thoroughfare the exterior is not particularly prepossessing, and is in fact more reminiscent

of an English pub than a decent hotel. But this is all part of the old-fashioned, Gamla Stan package – inside, things are different. One of the narrowest lobbies in Stockholm is full to overflowing, as with its sister hotels, with old models of ships, compasses and naval antiques. This theme is fervently maintained throughout the 29 rooms. These cabin-like constructions boast portholes and are named after famous ships. Rooftop decking offers respite from the slightly cramped interior, affording views over the ancient neighbourhood rooftops. Reasonable rates for the Old Town and heaps of character make this cosy set-up an attractive prospect.

Style 7, Atmosphere 7, Location 8

Lydmar Hotel, Sturegatan 10, Östermalm.
Tel: 566 113 00 www.lydmar.se
Rates: 1,235–1,950kr

The Lydmar is certainly distinctive in style, but its interior design might not be up everyone's street. The colour scheme is over-whelmingly dark, only saved from nigh-on Gothic by inspired design. All its 62 bedrooms have an arty feel, whether it's mono-

chrome minimalism or bright orange walls and opulent fabrics, and the bar downstairs hosts frequent live gigs. Music is the real feature here, from the artists who pick the Lydmar for its ultra-cool vibe, to the lift where you can choose anything from funk to jazz to accompany you up to bed. The hotel does not impress with extravagance – although rates are still high – but with its overall ambience of cool, from the rooms to the fantastic Lydmar restaurant. Here you escape the blackness, which is replaced by pink strip-lighting and upside-down models of reindeers on stark white walls.

Style 8, Atmosphere 7, Location 9

Nordic Light, Vasaplan, Box 884, Norrmalm.
Tel: 505 630 00 www.nordichotels.se
Rates: 2,470–3,510kr

One half of the Nordic Hotel pairing in Stockholm, this had once been hyped as the design hotel in the city – now it does exactly what it says on the packet. Stark and minimalist, the decorative interest is created by the use of light. The spacious, high-ceilinged lobby's blank white walls are used as a canvas for the continually shifting hues that characterize the times of day, and serve to break up the otherwise barren space. The rooms enjoy a similar feel, except as the customer it is up to you to adjust the light projections to your requirements (hearts for romance, etc.). Situated next to Central Station, it is a haven for business travellers arriving off the Arlanda Express, so expect groups of suited

men huddled around laptops in the hotel's communal areas. During the week, the environment is predominantly corporate, but at the weekends the more sophisticated travellers move in.

Although there's not much to speak of locally, the best bars and restaurants in town are just a short taxi-ride away.

Style 9, Atmosphere 7, Location 7

Nordic Sea, Vasaplan, Box 884, Norrmalm.
Tel: 505 630 00 www.nordichotels.se
Rates: 1,274–3,510kr

The little sister of Nordic Light, the Nordic Sea is not as style-conscious and caters more for the travelling businessman. Located next door to Central Station, it provides the ideal

stopover for those on their way in and out of town. As one might expect, the hotel's decorative theme is the sea rather than light; the colours are predominantly blue and white, and the furniture and design more conventional, as it relies on the simplicity of materials to create a relaxed and refined environment. Having said that, its biggest attraction is extraordinary. This is the Ice Bar, where you have to wear moon boots and fur-lined parkas to cope with the constant −10°C. The walls are made of ice, the tables are made of ice, the stools are made of ice and, yes, you drink chilled vodka out of ice glasses. The bar draws the tourists and the inquisitive, while the hotel maintains high standards of comfort and supplies all the expected mod-cons for the more sophisticated traveller.

Style 6, Atmosphere 6, Location 7

Radisson SAS Royal Park, Frosundaviks Alle 15, Box 3005, Solna.
Tel: 624 55 00 www.radissonsas.com
Rates: 1,230–5,000kr

This is another great example of Stockholm's 'countryside in the city'. Set in the suburb of Solna, the Radisson Royal Park is only a 20-minute drive from the centre of town but is surrounded by greenery. Inside, the hotel is breezy and fresh, and wooden floors and summery colours create a bright and airy mood. Its atmosphere is enhanced by the presence of the Sturebadet Haga spa, sister to Sturegallerian's Sturebadet (see page 201). Luxurious and emanating tranquillity, this encompasses the usual gym, pool and beauty treatments, all of an excellent standard. For exercise outdoors, a hearty walk in nearby Haga Park should satisfy the most energetic guest. Both businessmen and those in need of peaceful relaxation can enjoy this Radisson, which is certainly far superior to your average chain hotel.

Style 8, Atmosphere 7, Location 9

Radisson SAS Royal Viking Hotel, Vasagatan 1, Norrmalm.
Tel: 506 540 00 www.radisson.com
Rates: 975–1,700kr

Just a couple of minutes' walk from the Central Station, the second of the Radisson hotels is known for its practicality rather than its design. Its position in the centre of Norrmalm has obvious advantages for the business fraternity, but it is not bland, as so many business hotels can be. The suites are luxurious, equipped with their own private saunas, and are intriguingly

decorated (photographs of Madonna ingrained into the backs of chairs, for example). The standard rooms, however, are uninteresting although equipped with everything that you might possibly need. In the basement is the Bermuda Club, a health club and spa that has been designed in an 'authentic' Caribbean manner. The atmospheric pool area and jacuzzi are set beside a standard gym and small treatment centre. To get the most out of the hotel book into a suite and treat yourself to a sauna and jacuzzi before heading out to one of Stockholm's more stylish restaurants.

Style 7, Atmosphere 6, Location 8

Radisson SAS Strand, Nybrokajen 9, Östermalm.
Tel: 50 66 4000 www.radisson.com
Rates: 1,170–6,955kr

Despite being part of a large Scandinavian hotel chain, the Strand nevertheless stands out from the crowd, and closely rivals the nearby Grand. Its waterfront view is equally breathtaking, the suites almost as lavish and the rates marginally less exorbitant. The lobby, with its deep green leather armchairs and shelves stacked with books, sets the tone for the rest of the building, while the excellent restaurant looks up into the atrium. Radisson restaurants are always renowned for their superb quality, while their décor is often more individual than other branded chains. Here the Swedish influence is evident throughout, from the simplicity of the furniture to the nautical colour schemes. The suites are famous for their quality, with the aptly named Tower Suite offering magnificent views over the harbour and islands.

Style 8, Atmosphere 7, Location 9

Rica City Hotel Gamla Stan, Lilla Nygatan 25, Gamla Stan.
Tel: 723 7250 www.rica.se
Rates: 910–1,950kr

A few yards from the Lord Nelson, this Old Town favourite seems a lot more spacious because of its lack of clutter. Instead, it has a fresh atmosphere, with blue-and-white-checked curtains,

iron bed-heads and elegant suites decorated in an 18th-century style. Although it is comfortable and easy on the eye, its main appeal is its location. The cobbled streets of Gamla Stan are just beneath your window, the waterfront is a short walk away and with it the joys of Stockholm's best sights. In addition, both Mistral (**see page 116**) and Markattan (**see page 115**), two of the city's trendiest bars, are nearby, puncturing the area's touristy image. Snugly tucked away, but on the brink of being part of the party, this Rica City is pleasantly surprising.

Style 8, Atmosphere 7, Location 8

Rica City Hotel Stockholm, Slöjdgatan 7, Vasastan.
Tel: 723 72 00 www.rica.se
Rates: 910–1,885kr

Overlooking Hötorget's market and old concert hall, this is another product of the Rica City brand, saved from chain hotel monotony by several unique features. The best of these is the Vinterträdgården, or Winter Garden, where, surrounded by prettily frosted plants and trees, you can enjoy breakfast and look up into the hotel atrium. Here, rooms have been designed with the intention of breaking away from any possible blandness. In addition to this, its central location has a lot to offer. The main concert hall frequently stages interesting concerts, the market offers a genuine Stockholm experience and the huge cinema complex next door is always an option for a rainy day. The best jazz club in Stockholm, the well-known Fasching, is around the corner and

you can shop till you drop in a wide range of stores just on the hotel's doorstep.

> **Style 6, Atmosphere 6, Location 8**

● **Rival AB, Mariatorget 3, Södermalm.**
Tel: 545 789 00 www.rival.se
Rates: 2,275–2,795kr

Owned by a trio of high-powered local figures, including Benny from ABBA, this boutique hotel is a complex within itself: as well

as its 99 rooms, it incorporates a refurbished cinema, cocktail bar, café and bakery. Film plays an important part in the décor: every room is kitted out with a still taken from a classic Swedish movie, although the cinematically themed carpets do leave a little to be desired. Classic pieces of Nordic design, fantastic Egyptian linens and a 'pillow menu' are little extras for the patrons; the rooms are equipped with plasma screens and DVD players and the hotel's extensive DVD library renders trips to the cinema somewhat superfluous. Of the hotel's rooms the two penthouse suites are the most highly recommended and, compared with the local competition, far more reasonably priced. The Rival oozes modernity with shades of Greta Garbo.

> **Style 9, Atmosphere 8, Location 7**

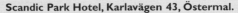

Scandic Park Hotel, Karlavägen 43, Östermal.
Tel: 517 348 00 www.scandic-hotels.se/park
Rates: 1,300–2,340kr

The Park hotels, as a chain, are always regarded as better than most, and that's certainly the case here. The Scandic adheres in some ways to the brand prototype, but its fantastic location and standard of accommodation put it a cut above the rest. Two minutes' walk from Stureplan, the hotel sits on a corner of Karlavägen with every possible bar, restaurant, club and department store practically on its doorstep. Inside, its brasserie is

good for breakfast or a mid-morning snack, and the lobby is warm and inviting. Rooms are comfortable although rather uniform – splash out on a suite if you're looking for more originality in design. A well-equipped fitness centre houses a good gym and male/female saunas. Good facilities and high levels of comfort are bonuses, but the big feature here is the hotel's address.

Style 6, Atmosphere 7, Location 9

Skepparholmen, Franckes väg, S-132 39 Saltsjö-Boo.
Tel: 747 65 00 www.skepparholmen.se
Rates: 975–1,625kr

Skepparholmen's excellent reputation relies heavily on its blissful

spa (**see page 202**), but the hotel has other attractions.
Bedrooms offer spectacular views of the archipelago and the

boating activities on the water through floor-to-ceiling windows.
A 1960s-inspired lobby is huge and unexciting but the warm
atmosphere and tastefully coloured rooms more than make up
for this. It's most fun in the summer when you can go to and fro
by boat between the hotel and Stockholm city centre in just 15
minutes. The hotel restaurant is agreeable but by venturing out
you'll see more of the countryside and town. However, if you've
come here more for the joys of a Swedish massage than anything
else, you will only need to trip down a few steps to immerse
yourself in the luxury of Skepparholmen's spa.

Style 7, Atmosphere 7, Location 8

Smådalarö Gård, Dalarö 130 54.
Tel: 501 551 00 www.smadalarogard.se
Rates: 1,170–2,470kr

This hotel is one of the furthest from the centre of Stockholm,
although a 45-minute drive doesn't exactly constitute a serious
mission. Situated out in the archipelago, the traditional manor
house is beautifully set in a rambling country estate. Within this,
the facilities, from a golf course to several tennis courts and of
course a programme of boating activities, make the hotel perfect

for a fan of country pursuits. During the winter businessmen fill
the rooms, but the summer months are reserved more for those

wanting to relax and enjoy the scenery. Nevertheless, for a
romantic break, the open fireplaces and snug rooms make this a
cosy getaway at any time of year. Unless you're going for one of
the Michelin-starred establishments, the city centre is a little far
for dinner, but classic Swedish fare is offered at the hotel's first-
rate restaurant. Smådalarö Gård's wood-fired sauna is also
heaven.

Style 8, Atmosphere 8, Location 8

Stallmästaregården, Norrtull, 113 47.
Tel: 610 13 00 www.stallmästaregården.se
Rates: 1,040–4,680kr

Another hotel set in stunning landscape, Stallmästargården combines classic and contemporary design. Although your first
impressions will be of a grand country hotel, with chandeliers
and period portraits decorating the reception area, the rooms
are in complete contrast to this. Most have a touch of the
Orient, whether in their art or furniture, and each is different in
some way from the next. Bold modern colours change the mood
from the hotel's initial formality to something cool and relaxed.

Quilt covers are made of silky fabric and bathrooms are spacious and generously endowed with prettily packaged products. Many rooms incorporate a downstairs sitting room fitted with top-of-the-range TVs and hi-fis. The top-class restaurant keeps crowds travelling here from near and far – in fact, for everything from a good walk to the best cuisine, you'll hardly have to move out of the grounds.

Style 9, Atmosphere 8, Location 8

The Victory, Lilla Nygatan 5, Gamla Stan.
Tel: 506 400 00 www.lady-hamilton.se
Rates: 1,235–5,785kr

The third and most upmarket of the Bengtsson hotels, The Victory has air of sophistication that is more noticeable than the down-to-earth charm of the Lord Nelson and the Lady Hamilton. The prevalence of nautical knick-knacks remains, but here the rooms are named after Swedish sea captains. The suites are wildly opulent: huge four-poster beds dominate softly lit bed-rooms leading off graceful sitting rooms, and manage to combine 17th-century elegance with Bang & Olufsen TVs and hi-fis. If you find yourself unable to move far from such luxury, no problem: the Leijontornet restaurant downstairs is decadent enough to keep you in the style to which you have just become accustomed. The excellent wine cellar sits among the remains of Stockholm's fortification walls. This hotel offers sheer indulgence in the middle of Gamla Stan's traditional charm.

Style 8, Atmosphere 9, Location 8

Villa Källhagen, Djurgårdsbrunnsvägen 10, Djurgården.
Tel: 665 03 00 www.kallhagen.se
Rates: 910–2,990kr

Villa Källhagen is perfectly placed, hidden away in Djurgården, Stockholm's city park. A stroll along the canal is just on your doorstep, but if a party is more your scene note that you will find plenty of entertainment available on the other side of the Djurgården Bridge. This is an intimate little place with a small

number of rooms, but lots of love and attention has been devoted to each. Rooms are light and rustic, and they all have panoramic views of the park. If you're happier amid the surrounding greenery than the nearby city hubbub, you'll be delighted to discover that the standards of food in the two restaurants dispense with the need to venture out elsewhere. Stockholm's businessmen bring clients here for a scenic lunch in either the à la carte dining room or the brasserie, and the food warrants its popularity. Eat plenty of whatever's on offer, whether traditional Swedish dishes or Italian pasta, safe in the knowledge that an energetic walk, post-lunch, will work it all off.

Style 8, Atmosphere 8, Location 9

Updates and notes...

eat...

Stockholm's residents take their food very seriously. And so they should: this city produces nothing less than a gourmet's paradise in terms of choice and quality of cuisine. The Swedes travel a lot, and their appreciation of diversity is reflected in the range and fusion of food on offer here. Ask a local what they consider to be a traditional 'Swedish' dish and they'll respond with a rather baffled expression and a pause as they think of an answer. At a push you might hear 'herrings', 'reindeer' or 'meatballs', on which many restaurants have their individual take.

Generally, however, restaurants in Stockholm describe their kitchens as offering a 'cross-over' menu – an international hybrid of more established European cuisines – and this seems to work. Of course, in amongst this fusion of tastes, you will find many places to eat which specialize in Oriental, Middle Eastern or Italian food but at the same time offer something a little more individual.

In addition to the range of choice, Stockholm has several restaurants whose cuisine puts them in a different class. There's a number that boasts one or more Michelin stars, among them Edsbacka Krog, Operakällaren and Fredsgatan 12. These, for obvious reasons, cost a little more than average, but are undoubtedly worth it. There are ways of getting round spending a fortune, however. Fredsgatan 12, for example, offers a set lunch at a very reasonable price and you'll experience the same delicious food.

Stockholm is a seasonal city – in the warm summer months the emphasis is on sitting outside, eating lightly and sipping some fine white wine. When winter rolls in, the temperatures plummet and everybody crowds indoors to sit close to roaring fires and feast on gamier meats, washed down with heavy red wine. This seasonality means that some places change, almost unrecognizably at times, from season to season. Menus alter as fish and seafood make way for heartier fare and warming staples.

The Swedish have a love of novelty, and new restaurants open up with alarming regularity, each offering a new concept or a different take on an established theme. This keeps the scene innovative and vibrant. As to when you can or should eat, there is really no strict pattern. Lunch begins at around 11.30am and goes on until 2.30pm, and most kitchens are open for supper between 5pm and 11pm.

During the week you might find that some of the restaurants seem to be rather quiet and forlorn. This is partly because the Swedes tend to eat at home with family and friends. The need to go out comes into force at weekends, but even then many people will stay at home until around midnight, when they'll hit the clubs. This is not to say that from Monday to Thursday you'll find places empty or populated entirely by tourists, but just that the weekend is when you'll feel the most authentic Stockholm vibe.

The restaurants are rated for their quality of food, the service and the atmosphere. The price given is the cost of two courses and half a bottle of wine for one.

Our top ten restaurants in Stockholm are:
1. Edsbacka Krog
2. Operakällaren
3. Wedholms Fisk
4. Pontus in the Greenhouse
5. Franka Matsalen
6. Berns Salonger
7. PA & Co
8. Bon Lloc
9. Fredsgatan 12
10. Riche

Our top five restaurants for food are:
1. Edsbacka Krog
2. Operakällaren
3. Bon Lloc
4, Restaurangen
5. Wedholms Fisk

Our top five restaurants for service are:
1. Operakällaren
2. Edsbacka Krog
3. Wedholms Fisk
4. Franska Matsalen
5. Pontus in the Greenhouse

Our top five restaurants for atmosphere are:
1. Berns Salonger
2. East
3. Edsbacka Krog
4. Grill
5. Riche

Bakfickan, Kungliga, Operan, Karl XIIs Torg, Norrmalm.
Tel: 676 58 09 www.operakallaren.se/bakfickan.cfm
Open: 11.30am–11.30pm. Closed Sunday.   260kr

Part of the Opera House dining 'empire', this is the most relaxed of all the restaurants, serving food until 11.30pm for those who want a better class of late-night munchies. With its dark-green lampshades and white tiles, it looks like a typical oyster bar, serving everything from oysters to traditional Swedish meatballs at the usual high Östermalm prices. It's at its most interesting just after an opera performance, when you will find exhausted sopranos discussing their last aria, while a less inspiring bankers' crowd fills the counter at lunchtime. Hidden away behind Café Opera (see page 153) and Operabaren (see page 118), it is perfect for a quick lunch or seriously good late-night snack before you creep back into Operabaren to relax in comfier surroundings.

Food 7, Service 8, Atmosphere 7

Berns Salonger, Berzelii Park, Norrmalm.
Tel: 566 322 22 www.berns.se
Open: 11.30am–3pm, 5pm–1am (4am Friday–Saturday).
Closed Sunday, and Monday dinner.   600kr

Terence Conran's influence is apparent as soon as you walk

through the door at Berns, and again when your food hits the table. The pure opulence of the dining room makes it a must, as does the quality of food that both Conran and Berns, as an independent restaurant, have become popular for. The huge room, with frescoed walls, high ceilings, chandeliers and softly lit tables, perfectly suits the clientele – a mix of Stockholm's elite, wealthy travellers staying in the Berns Hotel next door, and of course the odd international superstar. While seafood is a speciality, Berns also offers more traditional fare and steaks for those who like their meat. The food is fabulous, although predictably expensive given the historical surroundings and very civilized company. Stick around for a sharp contrast on Fridays, especially, in the form of wild partying from both next door and downstairs. Otherwise take time to appreciate the food and atmosphere without the pressures of the painfully cool Berns bar and club.

Food 8, Service 7, Atmosphere 9

Bistro Jarl, Birger Jarlsgatan 7, Östermalm.
Tel: 611 76 30 www.bistrojarl.se
Open: 11.30am–1am Monday–Friday; 1pm–2am Saturday.
Closed Sunday.   400kr

Labelled as a 'champagne and cocktail bar', Bistro Jarl in fact operates as a sedate and classic restaurant, attracting a mish-mash of businessmen and young Östermalm socialites sipping champagne. The bar at the far end offers succour to the inevitable tourist seeking sustenance after excessive spending two doors down in Gucci. Owing to its central position the prices are substantial, but then you are just 2 minutes from the

trendiest bars or a romantic waterfront stroll. The weekday atmosphere is somewhat sober, but there's a definite buzz come the weekend. The specialities of the menu vary, but you'll find an eternally extravagant theme: *foie gras*, *carpaccio* or an elaborate *bavaroise* with arctic raspberries. The interior is equally ornate, with greens and golds, pillars and painted wood, chandeliers and champagne bottles stacked in mirrored cabinets. Reserve a table on Fridays and Saturdays and settle in, or eat early and nip across to Riche opposite for more boisterous adventures.

Food 7, Service 7, Atmosphere 7

Bistro Ruby, Österlånggatan 14, Gamla Stan.
Tel: 206 057 76 www.bistroruby.com
Open: restaurant 5–11pm daily; bar 5pm–1am daily   350kr

Although similar in many ways to its sister restaurant next door, this little bistro aims at something more sophisticated, concentrating primarily on French food with a Swedish twist. Book beforehand, especially at weekends, for those cosy dinner dates by candlelight. This is one of the few restaurants in Gamla Stan where you will avoid hordes of tourists and the dreaded red-checked tablecloths. Don't be put off by the English menu catering for tourists: this is primarily a local spot. Beware the enormous portions — ask for a fillet of char and you'll find yourself ploughing through most of the fish. Having said this, the food is deliciously indulgent and won't disappoint Francophiles. As with Grill Ruby, there is a Saturday brunch — bloody Marys and eggs Benedict on a warm summer afternoon in Gamla Stan are without parallel elsewhere in Stockholm.

Food 7, Service 7, Atmosphere 7

Bon Lloc, Regeringsgatan 111, Östermalm.
Tel: 660 60 60 www.bonlloc.nu
Open: 5–11pm. Closed Sunday and throughout July.   450kr

Since an impressive number of Stockholm eating establishments have one or more Michelin stars to their name, it's difficult to decide which is better than the next. Awarded one star, Bon Lloc has the added bonus of having won *Gourmet* magazine's prestigious Best Restaurant Award in 2002. Consequently Mathias Dahlgren's Spanish food comes neither cheaply nor easily, as you won't be able to book for the same day. Dahlgren is a perfectionist — his food is his art but his method of cooking is more about intense flavours than decorative presentation. Bon Lloc,

meaning 'a good place', is a Catalan name, but don't expect your average *tapas*. Starters such as bay shrimp marinated in garlic with fresh potato purée will exceed all expectations of archetypal Spanish cuisine. With room for only 40 covers, simple Mediterranean whitewashed walls and terracotta bowls overflowing with ripe tomatoes concentrate the mind on the food in front of you and not the décor. Regulars aren't fazed by the high prices and neither should you be, since they simply reflect the sheer quality of the meal.

Food 9, Service 8, Atmosphere 7/8

Clas På Hörnet, Surbrunnsgatan 20, Vasastan.
Tel: 16 51 36 www.claspahornet.com
Open: 11.30am–11.30pm Monday–Friday;
11am–midnight Saturday; noon–10pm Sunday.   330kr

Dating back to 1736, this little corner of Surbrunnsgatan breathes history – you can't imagine that it has changed at all in the last few centuries. If the place exudes tradition, with its intimate tables for two, fireplaces and low ceilings, so too does the food. This is down to its use of typical Swedish ingredients, carefully observed to produce generous servings of meatballs or hen pheasant. Given the endless cafés producing excellent snacks, this is one of the few restaurants in Stockholm that might be better for lunch rather than dinner. But don't expect to be up to much afterwards. Just gorge yourself on food that merits an acute attack of greed and collapse, hoping that dinner will be a light, and late, affair. Feel reassured in the knowledge that you are not alone, as old Stockholm regulars all around you will be adopting this policy.

Food 7, Service 7, Atmosphere 8

Divino, Karlavägen 28, Norrmalm.
Tel: 611 02 69 www.divino.se
Open: 6–11pm. Closed Sunday and throughout July.   520kr

Although there are a few relatively well-known Italian restau-

rants in Stockholm, the general view is that there is nothing as luxurious or decadent as Divino. This just oozes Italian spirit, from the over-exuberant manager who greets you, to the rich, unrelenting flavours in often remarkable combinations: for example, pasta, figs and *foie gras*. Its central location, great service and an ever-changing but impressive wine list may mean steep prices, but pleasingly you will feel your pennies have gone a long way. The décor is elegant, with cream walls encompassing dark wooden dining tables. Although space is at a premium, it doesn't feel overcrowded and frankly the room is the last thing you'll be concentrating on once you've tasted your starter. The truly special food draws the upper echelons of Swedish society.

Food 8, Service 8, Atmosphere 6

East, Stureplan 13, Östermalm.
Tel: 611 49 59 www.east-restaurang.se
Open: 11.30am–11.30pm Monday–Saturday;
5–11pm Sunday.   330kr

This starkly decorated, Japanese-inspired restaurant serves a great selection of sushi. Sushi is massively popular, and seems to have spread with a force greater than in any other city in Europe. This remains one of the most popular spots, with its central location just off Stureplan providing an easy place for friends to meet for sushi nibbles, or for larger parties of the

Östermalm crowd. Expect a cross-section of Oriental food, from Vietnamese to Thai and back to sushi, and all priced relatively reasonably. Small, *tapas*-like dishes mean that you will need to order a few. Rock-hard chairs or cushions on the floor mean that the philosophy is primarily 'eat and leave'. Lunch might therefore be the sensible option here, leaving the evening free for you to enjoy East's equally trendy bar.

Food 7, Service 6, Atmosphere 8

Edsbacka Krog, Sollentunav. 220, Sollentuna, Stockholm.
Tel: 96 33 00 www.edsbackakrog.se
Open: 11.30am–2.30pm, 5.30pm–midnight (but note:
opening times may vary). 700kr

Having dinner at Edsbacka Krog is a serious event in every sense. Book a table, and spoil yourself with the exquisite food and surroundings. Don't go before or after anything, but reserve

a whole night for Edsbacka, because if there's one place in Stockholm that deserves your time, it's here. Located in the suburb of Sollentuna, some 20 minutes from the centre by taxi, this is an unlikely site for a double Michelin-starred restaurant. Its exterior is reminiscent of a dilapidated country inn and on walking in this initial impression is, in a positive sense, confirmed, with open fireplaces and low-hanging beams. However, there is something tremendously reassuring about the way in which such a high-class restaurant manages to retain down-to-earth comfort. The Michelin awards speak for themselves where the Swedish/European food is concerned: the head chef and owner Christer Lindström is renowned for his ability to make a plate look so beautiful that it would be criminal actually to eat anything on it.

> **Food 10, Service 9, Atmosphere 8**

Eriks Bakficka, Fredrikshovsgatan 4, Östermalm.
Tel: 660 15 99 www.eriks.se
Open: 11.30am–midnight Monday–Friday;
5pm–midnight Saturday; 5–10pm Sunday.   350kr

Although still in the exclusive Östermalm district, Eriks Bakficka nestles in a more residential area than that surrounding the chic boutiques and bars of Stureplan. This brings in a clientele made up mostly of local regulars who know the menu by heart and will come to enjoy great food or a strong drink on a relaxed Sunday evening. This is catered for by a snug log-cabin-like dining area and the bar next door, which is cosily lit with traditional green lampshades. The menu is based on Scandinavian home-cooking and head chef Erik Lallerstedt can be spotted doing the rounds, to check that his herrings or crème brulée are up to scratch. Unwilling to follow nearby stylish trends, this restaurant

concentrates on exclusive food in traditional surroundings. Bakficka is the little sister of chef Erik's Gondolen (see page 77), but its low-key interior and mood have ensured that, unlike Gondolen, it has maintained an authentic Swedish atmosphere, undiscovered as yet by hordes of tourists.

Food 7, Service 7, Atmosphere 7

Folkhemmet, Renstiernas Gata 30, Södermalm.
Tel: 640 55 95 www.users.wineasy.se/folkhemmet
Open: 11am–2am daily   330kr

Another of Södermalm's trendsetters, Folkhemmet is set slightly out on a limb – and isn't afraid to say so in terms of its menu, either. The name has a political origin, and literally translates as

'the people's home'. Its living-room feel, with light wooden floors and dark-blue cushioned chairs, justifies this characterization. The 'F' in Folkhemmet steals its style from the city's 'T' for Tunnelbana on the signs for the metro; this association goes hand-in-hand with the arty, creative types that the restaurant tends to lure. No one bats an eyelid at such novel combinations as pike, perch and seafood risotto on the menu; indeed, the sophisticated clientele mirror the ingenuity of the chef. The food is hard to label definitively: Mediterranean? Swedish? Perhaps a bit of both, but, above all, Folkhemmet stays refreshingly clear of the homogenized tastes offered by so many other restaurants.

Food 7, Service 7, Atmosphere 8

Franska Matsalen, Grand Hotel, S. Blasieholmskajen 8, Östermalm.
Tel: 679 35 84 www.franskamatsalen.nu
Open: 6–11pm. Closed Saturday and Sunday.   650kr

Since it's part of the illustrious Grand Hotel, you'd expect this restaurant to live up to a fiercely defended one Michelin star reputation and, as a grand French treasure, it does not disappoint. As with the hotel, you are surrounded by typical old-world

glamour, both in terms of décor and people; plush, deep-red fabrics create a proper atmosphere for discerning regulars who know their Sevruga from their Beluga and their Burgundies from Bordeaux. Part of the restaurant's appeal is its location, so make sure you call and book a table on the waterfront where the experience of a palace view combined with gastronomic delight is almost unbeatable. Be prepared to splash out on dinner, as, with critics heaping more awards onto this place every year, the traditional Swedish and alternative French cuisine comes at a hefty price.

Fredsgatan 12, Fredsgatan 12, Norrmalm.
Tel: 24 80 52 www.fredsgatan12.com
Open: 11.30am–2pm, 5pm–1am. Closed Sunday.   500kr

It comes as no surprise that another member of the group that
includes the unconventional Grill (see page 78) and
Restaurangen (see page 90) also offers its own distinctive

approach to how food should be presented and consumed. The
overwhelming premise is extreme simplicity and cleanliness,
verging on minimalism, although the portions are substantial. The
award-winning food is exquisite: Light, Nature, Ocean, Meat and
Sweet – have one, three or all five of these mini courses and
treat your taste-buds to what is the modern equivalent of a
menu degustation. In the evening you'll find a sedate but mixed
crowd enjoying this, while at noon the less inspired market-
speak of businessmen runs counter to the neon colours of the
surrounding room. Bright yellow transparent sheaths cover huge
clear windows while improbable pink lamp-shades loom over the
scattered tables. Based in the centre of the banking district, it
offers little escape from the stiff business tone, but the inventive
décor and food which has won this restaurant *Guide Rouge* one-

star status is worth getting excited about, even if those around you only seem quietly enthusiastic.

Food 9, Service 8, Atmosphere 6

● **Fyra Knop, Svartensgatan 4, Södermalm.**
Tel: 640 77 27
Open: 5–11pm Monday–Friday;
11.30am–11pm Saturday–Sunday.   230kr

This is probably the most downtrodden restaurant included here, but it just had to get a mention. Restaurants in Stockholm, even on the corners of Södermalm, do not usually succeed in combining scruff with great food. More usually you get what you see, which is why most places are either trendy in the extreme or just very grand. This is neither, with peeling wallpaper, plastic orange menus only in Swedish and a generally crusty feel all round. The décor fits well with the slapdash although delicious crêpes and *galettes* that Fyra Knop exclusively serves. Food comes quickly and the *galettes* are filled with both simple and extraordinary fillings, so you'd better ask yourself how daring you're feeling. The crêpes are reserved for pudding and hold

everything from chocolate sauce to lashings of intoxicating liqueurs. A bohemian and alternative interior is fitting for the unorthodox crowd that frequents this spot. This crêperie is full of scrappy charm and although you need to look to find it, it is in fact easily accessible. Try to sit in the room furthest from the entrance if you eat here and you'll feel that everyone inside is just an extension of the furniture.

> **Food 7, Service 5, Atmosphere 7**

Gerda's, Östermalm's Saluhall, Humlegårdsgatan 1–3, Östermalm.
Tel: 553 404 40
Open: 9.30am–6pm Monday–Thursday;
9.30am–6.30pm Friday; 9.30am–4pm Saturday.   330kr

Gerda's sits next to Lisa Elmqvist (see page 83) in Saluhallen (the covered market) and the two work together, mopping up each other's overflow. They are very similar and equally popular, although perhaps because of the properly laid tables and napkin rings, Gerda's could be considered a tad more up-market. This small difference apart, the prices are almost identical, although

here you will have the table to yourself. There isn't a bar at Gerda's, so you'll have to pop in for lunch. The open kitchen is easily observed from wherever you sit, so you can keep an eye on everything from the fish-gutting to final preparation of your food. The real point, however, is to go to Saluhallen, whet your appetite by looking around, and sit down to confirm that the food really is as good as it looks in the stalls surrounding you.

Food 8, Service 6, Atmosphere 8

Goccia, Hamngatan 7, Norrmalm.
Tel: 611 25 22
Open: 11am–1am. Closed Sunday.   470kr

Before the recent opening of Goccia, Divino had little competition as far as seriously high-class Italian food was concerned.
Now, however, it may suffer slightly, as the Italian delicacies on
offer here more than match up to those of its rival. It's modern
in style; orange is the predominant colour, and coats the furniture and lampshades throughout the room. Chairs are art deco

and designed more for admiring than sitting on, but the rich
truffle-laced dishes and a style-conscious crowd are here more
important than comfort. Conspicuously located on a corner of
Hamngatan, and only yards from NK and Strandvagen, it attracts
an elite set, who expect good food to be accompanied by a chic
dining comapnions. This lot gather pre-dinner to decorate the
bar, where equally decorative cocktails are on offer. Alternatively
save this part of the Goccia experience for later, when authentic
Italian coffee will not disappoint the most fastidious of caffeine
addicts.

Food 7, Service 7, Atmosphere 7

Gondolen, Stadsgården 6, Södermalm.
Tel: 641 70 90 www.eriks.se
Open: 11.30am–1am Monday–Friday; 1pm–1am Saturday.
Closed Sunday.   490kr

The very idea of this gondola-like suspension 36 metres above ground is, unsurprisingly, a great draw for those visiting Stockholm. It remains popular with businessmen, who like to stage client meetings against the spectacular backdrop it provides, while few sightseers are able to resist the 5kr ride up to investigate this unlikely looking venue. The Gondolen owners are well aware of

their draw as far as tourists are concerned, and disappointingly have decorated it like a chain hotel. Patterned carpets and cushions have resulted in an overly kitsch interior, although some respite is offered in the wooden panelled bar where one can make the most of the views. The menu displays a typical international mix, but reindeer and herrings are all part of the effort to keep up the 'local' façade. There is a smaller kitchen section in the restaurant which offers cheaper but similar food in far simpler but authentic-looking surroundings. It's generally a sedate affair with a business feel at lunchtime and a mixture of tourists and businessmen in the evening, so it is probably wisest to take a drink here and follow it up with dinner close by. As it's located in Slussen, you'll have all of the Östermalm and Gamla Stan restaurants to choose from.

> **Food 7, Service 7, Atmosphere 6**

Grill, Drottninggatan 89, Norrmalm.
Tel: 31 45 30 www.grill.se
Open: 11.30am–2pm, 5pm–1am Monday–Friday;
5pm–1am Saturday; noon–5pm Sunday.   400kr

The managers here describe Grill as a restaurant with a 'living room' feel, but in fact it looks more like a modern furniture store. Although this sounds off-putting, in fact this place feels very homely, with its numerous different sofas, armchairs and tables scattered about the large room. The idea is to create

comfortable surroundings in which to collapse and enjoy a relaxed chat over a unique menu. The last third of the Restaurangen/Fredsgatan 12 group, it follows that Grill should be as original as its sister restaurants. Here the concept is to offer a menu of dishes where food is cooked in one of five ways – stone-baked, rotîsserie, barbecue, charcoal or *ishiyaki*. Fish, meat and vegetables are prepared in your preferred style and the extensive wine list is closely aligned with the menu, giving detailed recommendations as to what is best to drink with what. This is a new and cool establishment, but manages to achieve the cosiness it has set out to generate. Also, the food is exquisite.

Food 8, Service 7, Atmosphere 8

Grill Ruby, Österlånggatan 14, Gamla Stan.
Tel: 20 57 76 www.grillruby.com
Open: 5–11.30pm Monday–Friday; 1–5pm Saturday.   360kr

There are few restaurants in Stockhom that concentrate exclusively on the type of American staples at which this Gamla Stan spot excels. As a result, despite its location at the centre of the cobbled Old Town tourist trap, Grill Ruby is crammed with locals. The Grill has no pretentiousness or affectation; instead it provides a haven for those trying to escape the airs and graces

of many restaurants in Östermalm, while remaining more up-market than the more alternative joints of Sodermalm. The local feel is reflected in the lack of an English menu – although don't worry about this, as a translation of 'sirloin' or 'fillet' shouldn't prove too testing. Décor is relaxed, and the mood warm and cosy: American movie posters featuring Bonnie and Clyde plaster the pale green wooden slatted walls, while Aretha Franklin plays in the background. Mix your meat and veg as you see fit, with the menu divided into clear sections to make life easier for all (although this does change slightly for Saturday brunch). At weekends it is best to book, but otherwise turn up with a newspaper, sit at the bar and wait your turn.

Food 8, Service 7, Atmosphere 7

Den Gyldene Freden, Österlånggatan 51, Gamla Stan.
Tel: 24 97 60 www.gyldenefreden.se
Open: 6–11pm Monday–Friday; 1–11pm Saturday.
Closed Sunday. 450kr

Despite its rustic air – think wooden beams, candlelit tables and the ghosts of Swedish poets – Den Gyldene Freden is, thankfully, not another of Gamla Stan's cosy but unexciting bistros. Renowned across Stockholm for its sumptuous, rich-bordering-on-heavy food, it is best avoided if you're dieting. The calves' liver comes with thick gravy while the puddings are packed with cream and several days' RDA of calories. On a freezing winter's evening it is the epitome of comfort and warmth. Just yards away

on this main Gamla Stan street is a handful of other gems, including Grill and Bistro Ruby and Pontus in the Greenhouse. The Gamla Stan location in itself is enough to guarantee the odd tourist or two, but it's worth suffering them for the delicious

Swedish/French food. Prices are high, but not quite in the same league as Pontus. If you're after a simple and comfortable evening, try drinks and olives in the Greenhouse bar before a stroll along the cobbles to Den Gyldene Freden.

> **Food 7, Service 6, Atmosphere 8**

Haga Forum, Annerovägen 4, Solna.
Tel: 33 48 44
Open: 11.30am–3pm Monday; 11.30am–11pm Tuesday–Friday;
noon–11pm Saturday.   300kr

This odd-looking place was built as the SAS headquarters but was subsequently converted to the Haga terminal, an area reserved for passengers at Arlanda airport. Now, however, it's a very trendy restaurant. Don't be put off by its ugly grey exterior: inside, roaring fires and modern furniture warm the mood. It's particularly popular for Sunday brunch, so come and collapse comfortably onto a minimalist sofa and tuck into a steak or salad. Once inside, you'll discover that the view more than makes up for the uninspiring architecture. As the name suggests, the

restaurant enjoys picturesque vistas of the water and greenery of Haga Park. Business lunches fill the place at noon, but these are generally informal and don't intrude on the relaxed atmosphere. If you to choose to come for lunch, round it off with a brief walk in the park. This restaurant is on the edge of town, so catch a taxi for a hassle-free experience.

Food 7, Service 7, Atmosphere 8

Halv Grek Plus Turk, Jungfrugatan 33, Östermalm.
Tel: 665 94 22 www.halvgrekplusturk.com
Open: 5.30pm–midnight Monday–Saturday;
5.30–11.30pm Sunday.   460kr

A successful experiment and another example of Stockholm's openness to all things gastronomically alternative, Halv Grek Plus Turk combines Greek with Turkish cuisine, as its name suggests. The result is a juxtaposition of the traditional with the innovative and exotic, and a reputation that makes booking essential, particularly at weekends. Eastern Mediterranean décor is achieved with mirrored cushions and blue finishes on walls and furniture, giving the main restaurant a Greek island feel. Next door, there is a small bar with miniature light-blue mosaic tiles covering the walls and lighting provided by Moroccan-inspired shades and lanterns. It's worth going in just for a cocktail, but the

food deserves plenty of attention, too, if you have a tastse for the unusual. This place is interesting from every angle, and this includes the diverse crowd, all of whom are here to eat something less ordinary than the continental 'cross-over' fare offered in so many of Stockholm's restaurants.

Food 7, Service 7, Atmosphere 8

Hotellet, Linnégatan 18, Östermalm.
Tel: 442 89 00
Open: 5pm–1am. Closed Sunday.   360kr

Hotellet opened in 2003, and has since then successfully attracted its clientele with its unusual approach to its menu. Divided into different sections – meat, fish, vegetables, sauces and side orders – the menu allows you to create your own meal. Simply choose a basic ingredient and combine it with a sauce and side dish, and *voilà*. Experience, for example, the taste sensations of tuna Bordelaise or truffled spinach. The essence is the simplicity of choice for both customer and kitchen. Located among all the action in Östermalm, the restaurant is in competition with the likes of East and Riche for the attention of some of the more chic local residents. The excellent bar and garden filled with art-deco furniture make it a fixture for both balmy summer evenings and long winter nights.

Food 7, Service 7, Atmosphere 7

Koh Phangan, Skånegatan 57, Södermalm.
Tel: 642 68 65
Open 5pm–1am. Closed Sunday. 330kr

Initial impressions are often the most important, and here at
Koh Phangan they definitely verge on the kitsch. Looking like it
has been transplanted straight from the islands of southern
Thailand, the neon-lit bar emits a strange ultraviolet glow, high-
lighting the cushioned alcoves. The ubiquitous presence of Bob

Marley and bad euro-pop in Koh Samui also re-emerges here.
The only thing truly lacking is a ladyboy offering to love you 'long
time'. Despite all this, it does serve up healthy portions of
cleansing Thai cuisine at a reasonable price. The clientele remi-
nisce about their experiences in Bangkok or aspire to gain some
– they sit on scruffy benches sipping inventive cocktails before
wandering across the bridges that span the small pools of water
to reach their table. The late licence at weekends ensures a
buzzing atmosphere full of kindred bohemian spirits.

Food 8, Service 6, Atmosphere 8

**Lisa Elmqvist, Östermalm's Saluhall, Humlegårdsgatan
1–3, Östermalm.**
Tel: 553 40 400 www.lisaelmqvist.se
Open: 9.30am–6pm Monday–Thursday; 9.30am–6.30pm Friday;
9.30am–4pm Saturday. 330kr

Lisa Elmqvist is an experience for the real foodies among us, situated as it is at the centre of Saluhallen, the most impressive food market in Stockholm. You could spend most of the morning here salivating over everything from the freshest fish to the most decadent chocolate cake, before settling down to eat. Since it is less a restaurant than a place to enjoy the smells and tastes of everything around you, it is hard to say whether you are best off sticking with a simple plate of *gravadlax* or going full pelt into enormous portions of sole or sea bass. Whatever you choose, the highest quality is guaranteed. Eating here is not a formal affair; be prepared to share your table with a couple of other diners if your party doesn't fill all the chairs, since this place is too popular for the management to grant privacy. Prices vary according to market forces – this is not Wedholms Fisk, although you wouldn't know it from the standard of the food.

Food 7, Service 6, Atmosphere 8

Mooncake, Luntmakargatan 95, Norrmalm.
Tel: 16 99 28 www.mooncake.se
Open: 5pm–midnight Monday–Friday; 5–10pm Sunday.   450kr

A cool variant on Oriental cuisine in the small Chinatown-like area of Stockholm. Hidden away two doors down from the highly suspect strip-club Kino, it can be quite hard to find. As a result, at the beginning of the week the place is pretty empty, but this is no reflection on the standard of food. The kitchen has given standard Chinese, Vietnamese and Thai dishes its own 'Swedish' twist. Forget ordering lots of little courses, as you might in a traditional Chinese establishment. Here, one portion of Peking Duck will suffice, accessories included, arranged in such a way that you feel like you've had a whole meal rather than one part of it. The décor is simple verging on stark, with one black and white photo of Vietnam dominating the white room. No high-pitched Oriental music but soft jazz, which suits the altogether chilled-out and quietly fashionable mood.

Food 8, Service 7, Atmosphere 7

Operakällaren, Operahuset, Karl XII's torg, Norrmalm.
Tel: 676 58 00 www.operakallaren.se
Open: 11.30am–3am Monday–Friday; 1pm–3am Saturday. 700kr

The ultimate in old-fashioned romance, Operakällaren's Michelin star brings in couples from Stockholm and beyond, for hushed, romantic conversations. Ella Fitzgerald sings softly in the background, while in the winter a roaring fire at one end of the large dining room makes the mood even more intimate. The décor is grand: paintings of Aphrodite line the ceiling while diners sink into deep red velvet-cushioned chairs. Older regulars smoke cigars in the adjoining conservatory, where the view over the water is stunning. Finding the odd tourist here is a certainty, since Operakällaren's reputation precedes it all over the world. However, prices will deter all but the most generous high-flyers, so expect to dine in highly sophisticated company. Having resigned oneself to an expensive evening, it is worth splashing out on the *menu degustation*. Wines specially selected to accompany each of the spectacular seven courses will ensure you get the best from the Operakällaren experience.

Food 9, Service 9, Atmosphere 8

PA & Co, Riddargatan 8, Östermalm.
Tel: 611 08 45
Open: 5pm–midnight daily   320kr

Few guidebooks mention this little jewel, since its most fashionable era seems to have passed. However, for those who come here for the local ambience and earthy food rather than to see and be seen, it remains hugely popular. This is a bonus, since Stockholm regulars now make up the majority of the crowd and visit often to enjoy the consistently high-quality cuisine; this includes dishes from Caesar salad to reindeer. With the menu scrawled in chalk across a raised blackboard, décor is simple although there has been an effort to retain traditional features such as an old but working cigarette machine and battered wood-

en benches around the tables. Situated on Riddargatan, it is minutes from the more trendy bars and restaurants, so if you've seen enough of the down-to-earth side of Östermalm by the end of dinner, the more stylish establishments are just down the road.

Food 8, Service 8, Atmosphere 8

Pontus' Brasserie by the Sea, Tullhus 2, Skeppsbrokajen, Gamla Stan.
Tel: 20 20 95 www.pontusfrithiof.com
Open: 4pm–1am. Closed Sunday, October–April.   500kr

The summertime alternative to Pontus in the Greenhouse, this is

the second of the two restaurants to be named after their chef. As you'd expect, it sits right on the waterfront, but it is closed in the winter since it's just too cold to eat in the marquee-like construction. Given a warm summer's day, however, freshly caught seafood is enjoyed by a cool crowd uniformly sporting sunglasses and daintily picking at crayfish and lobster. Wicker chairs are comfortable and appropriate for the light and airy surroundings, and the décor otherwise is simple and primarily of neutral colour. Pontus by the Sea has an impressive reputation in Stockholm and prices to suit, although it's perhaps not on the scale of Pontus in the Greenhouse, since this restaurant is more in keeping with lunchtime affairs than indulgent three-course dinners.

Food 8, Service 7, Atmosphere 8

Pontus in the Greenhouse, Österlånggatan 17, Gamla Stan.
Tel: 24 25 32 www.pontusfrithiof.com
Open: 11.30am–3pm, 6–11pm. Closed Sunday lunch.   680kr

Here you'll find some of the best food in Stockholm – that is, if you can work your way around the set menus, both classic and modern, and negotiate the à la carte. There is also a separate bar menu that gives you the option of some lighter dishes. The interior of the bar has to be one of the 'snuggest' in the city, with deep sofas and rich colours reminiscent of heather-clad hills.

Upstairs there is more formal dining with old-fashioned red-cushioned seats and glittering table settings that make it seem timeless. The food is exceptional and the young chef has created a gastronomic experience that is admired throughout Stockholm's culinary community. The wine list is definitive, with the sommelier very protective of its contents: he would not allow the secrets of the cellar to leave the restaurant with us!

Food 8, Service 8, Atmosphere 8

Restaurangen, Oxtorgsgatan 14, Norrmalm.
Tel: 22 09 52 www.restaurangentm.com
Open: 11.30am–2pm, 5pm–1am.
Closed Saturday lunch and Sunday.   460kr

Although its inconspicuous location and dirty green walls are hardly enticing, Restaurangen has hidden depths. This, the third restaurant from the Grill stable (see page 78), manages to hit the heights that the previous two have so far failed to attain. Here, it is the food and concept that make the restaurant unique. Mark off your chosen dishes on the menu with a pencil – there are set prices for the number of dishes you order. Wines to complement the dishes are listed next to them. The food is delicious but the portions do tend to be small, so order more than you might usually. At lunchtime the atmosphere is more business-like, while the clever use of lighting in the evening makes the drab interior seem more intimate.

Food 9, Service 7, Atmosphere 6

Restaurang Prinsen, Mäster Samuelsgatan 4, Östermalm.
Tel: 611 13 11 www.restaurangprinsen.se
Open: 11.30am–11.30pm Monday–Friday;
1–11.30pm Saturday; 5–10.30pm Sunday.   390kr

Located just off the exclusive Biblioteksgatan, Restaurang Prinsen has long been a lunchtime haunt for weary shoppers. In fact, this

small bistro has been serving everything from scampi and shrimp salad to the classic 'Biff Rydberg' since 1897. This is evident in the old-fashioned décor – leather-covered banquettes, dark wooden slats and framed pictures of Swedish notaries. In addition, waiters are dressed top-to-toe in starched white uniforms and most have been there as long as the restaurant. Lunchtime offers brasserie-type choices, while an à la carte menu is more ambitious for dinner. Whatever you choose, you will have got your kroner's worth, as the food is influenced heavily by Scandinavian tradition. A quick Toast Pelle Jansson (raw fillet of beef, whitebait roe and red onion) will make a perfect lunchtime snack to energize you for further shopping nearby. In keeping with its old-fashinoned style the service is exemplary, if slightly formal.

Food 7, Service 8, Atmosphere 7

Riche, Birger Jarlsgatan 4, Östermalm.
Tel: 679 68 42 www.riche.se
Open: 11.30am–2.30am Monday–Saturday;
1–10pm Sunday.   410kr

One of Stockholm's über-fashionable bar/restaurants, appealing to the young and beautiful. Riche is not a place for an intimate evening; instead it sets a frenetic pace as groups of friends jostle for a space

at the bar and hassle the waiters for tables. The modern décor, with interesting lamps and furniture, lends an elegance to the place that is mirrored in the clientele. The food, while not the best in town, is still of a high standard, but it is the atmosphere that sets this restaurant apart. Thursday nights in particular inspire an enthusiastic crowd to eat, chat and prepare for a long night dancing the night away in the nearby Kharma or Lydmar. The menu is a fusion of Swedish and European fare, creating a highly palatable if slightly uninspiring choice. You are here most of all to see and be seen.

Food 7, Service 6, Atmosphere 8

Lo Scudetto, Åsögatan 163, Södermalm.
Tel: 640 42 15 www.loscudetto.se
Open: 5pm–midnight. Closed Sunday.   390kr

This Södermalm Italian is hidden away in one of south
Stockholm's dingier streets, but is worth seeking out. Less obviously exclusive than Divino or Goccia, it serves ambitious food
in a low-key environment. Prices are more reasonable, since you

are paying just for delicious food and not (as in parts of Östermalm) for a particularly elite location or interior. Having said
this, there's little to criticize about the restaurant's design – with
plenty of candlelight and low ceilings, the overall feel is one of
warm relaxation and ease. Tiny, it crams in tables almost on top
of each other, but this is all part of the homely atmosphere, and
people are less interested in checking out others than enjoying
intimate conversations with their date. Pasta favourites, a relaxed
mood and reasonable prices make this a good alternative to
Östermalm's two Italians.

Food 7, Service 7, Atmosphere 6

Stiernan, Renstiernas Gata 22, Södermalm.
Tel: 643 97 33
Open: 5pm–1am daily. Closed Sunday.   400kr

You have to go further and search harder than in Östermalm to find the best restaurants in south Stockholm. This, along with a handful of others, is one worth seeking out. *Stiernan* means 'star' and as you walk in you'll be particularly struck by the décor: large blue star shapes hang from the ceiling and make an effective contrast with the bar's dark reds. Because of the colours, the restaurant takes on a cooler, calmer feel. This fits in well with the customers, who are either alternative Södermalm sorts or

Östermalm inhabitants who prefer to venture out of the mainstream spots. Although it describes its cuisine as 'European with a Swedish twist', this claim errs more on the Scandinavian side, with unusual combinations of flavours providing an exciting change to Stockholm's usual representation of the European/Swedish cross-over. The wickedly decadent bar gets packed to bursting over the weekend, with diners preferring to kick back here rather than traipsing further through Södermalm for late-night drinks.

Food 7, Service 8, Atmosphere 8

Teater Grillen, Nybrogatan 3, Östermalm.
Tel: 545 035 62 www.riche.se
Open: 11.30am–2.30pm, 5pm–1am. Closed Monday dinner, Saturday lunch and Sunday.   450kr

This side pocket of the glamorous Riche (see page 92) lives up to its name in terms of location, clientele and design. With its own entrance beside the Dramaten theatre, the restaurant fills up with enthusiastic theatre-goers and arty types who appreciate the themed interior. Theatrical masks adorn the walls above intimate red-cushioned niches, and equally decadent cuisine is served to an older crowd than in Riche. The food is excellent – lobster and oysters are typical fare, and their prices suit the wallets of the sophisticated diners. The theatrical spirit is all-pervasive, and many dishes are named after Dramaten actors. If you want to immerse yourself in this further and enjoy an extra slice of theatre history, you can book what was once Ingmar Bergman's private table.

Food 8, Service 7, Atmosphere 8

Tranan, Karlbergsvägen 14, Vasastan.
Tel: 527 281 00 www.tranan.se
Open: 11.30pm–1am Monday–Friday;
5pm–1am Saturday–Sunday.   290kr

'Quintessential Stockholm' is how regulars might refer to this spot. Unpretentious, from the red chequered tablecloths to the loud chatter of locals, Tranan draws a mixed crowd, attracted by the general hustle and bustle. It is unusual for a place to be regarded as 'cool' by such a diverse clientele, but from hip-hop suburban kids to elderly loners clutching a newspaper, this is a favourite. Plates come piled with mashed potatoes and steak or alternatively steaming bowls of mussels. Friendly, smiling waiters serve food from a menu they know by heart, and can talk you through every dish with great enthusiasm. The air is smoky, which might make it less appealing for some, but it does add to the *laissez-faire* attitude of the place. That said, it is sensible to book a table since, although relaxed, Tranan is tremendously popular. Very reasonable prices, comfort food at its best and an all-round buzz contribute to this, as does its downstairs bar, which deserves a write-up all of its own – (see page 121).

Food 7, Service 7, Atmosphere 8

Umami, Birger Jarlsgatan 25, Östermalm.
Tel: 411 14 02 www.umami.se
Open: 11.30am–11.30pm Monday–Friday;
6–11pm Saturday. Closed Sunday.   330kr

With sushi making its name as the most popular 'novelty' food in Stockholm, there is plenty of choice in terms of where to eat it. Umami, which takes its name from the elusive third flavour in the trio that includes 'hot' and 'sour', has branched out within this theme. The simple recipes combining all three food types result in clean-tasting dishes. Sushi is an option, but it is worth sampling the seared tuna or hot and sour Korean cabbage salad if you're feeling brave. The interior is very neat; presentation of everything from food to tableware is immaculate, and menus and even the bill come wrapped in origami envelopes. The chilled background beat and dark-brown wood contrasting with pink neon light makes this perfect for an early drink if the food isn't up your street – cocktails are helpfully divided into pre- and post-dinner sections. Otherwise go to Umami for a 'clean' Japanese-style supper and brush up on your chopstick skills as there isn't an alternative.

Food 8, Service 7, Atmosphere 7

Vassa Eggen, Birger Jarlsgatan 29, Östermalm.
Tel: 21 61 69 www.vassaeggen.com
Open: 11.30am–2pm, 5pm–1am.
Closed Saturday lunch and Sunday.   520kr

Chic from décor to clientele, Vassa Eggen ('Sharp Edge') lives up to its name. Savvy 30-somethings flock from nearby Stureplan, and elsewhere, for stylish surroundings and the company of a well-groomed crowd. Modern cooking has shades of the Mediterranean with a French twist and the food is rich and indulgent – *foie gras* is a staple on the interesting menu. The interior is elegant, waiters discreet and tables immaculately presented. The mood, however, is not stiff but informal, owing to the fashionable and street-wise professionals. The bar emits a funky glow which softens the otherwise minimalist décor, and attractive Stockholmers mill around clutching a cocktail before eating here or elsewhere. Fine dining at its best.

Food 8, Service 8, Atmosphere 7

Wedholms Fisk, Nybrokajen 17, Östermalm.
Tel: 611 78 74
Open: 11.30am–2pm, 6–11pm Monday;
11.30am–11pm Tuesday–Friday; 5–11pm Saturday.   600kr

As you'd expect in a city surrounded by water, there is some serious competition in the fight for best lobster, but with one Michelin star to its name, Wedholms Fisk must come pretty high up the list. Elegant and soothing, it's the place to enjoy beautifully prepared fish in civilized and sedate surroundings, and although it's popular with an older crowd, the quality of food brings in all ages. On a summer's day sit outside for lunch and take in the views of the waterfront, although dinner may be a better option if you want to avoid suited business lunches. A pale and understated décor is appropriate given the modestly dressed clientele.

Expect hushed tones in serious elegance, and come for the food – the only fireworks here are culinary.

Food 9, Service 9, Atmosphere 7

Zoe, Jungfrugatan 6, Östermalm.
Tel: 661 27 77 www.matsedel.com
Open: 11am–2pm Monday–Friday; 5–10pm Monday–Thursday;
5–11pm Friday–Saturday; 1–5pm Sunday.   360kr

Traditional restaurants packed with lots of 'Swedish' character are often seen as the preserve of the Old Town, where endless bistros cash in on the passing tour groups. It is worth seeking out Zoe, however, hidden away deep in the centre of town, for cosy evenings without Östermalm affectation. Deep-red walls and menus written on chalk-boards make this small eaterie feel justifiably real. The initial earthy impression is further enhanced by the restaurant's attitude. Unless your Swedish is somewhat above basic, you're unlikely to understand the menu, but listen to the very knowledgeable waiter's advice and you won't be disappointed. Thick chunks of bread come with a hefty wooden spatula for smearing on exciting tomato and garlic butter. Fish is the order of the day, arriving beautifully presented on huge white plates accompanied by robust side orders of beetroot and mashed potatoes. Try and save room for some of the richest puddings in town. The direct approach of waiters and unpretentious clientele are a breath of fresh air in a part of town better known for its exclusivity and haughtiness.

Food 7, Service 8, Atmosphere 8

drink . . .

The Swedes are very keen on their alcohol, so there are few places where you won't be able to get your favourite cocktail. Also bear in mind that most restaurants in Stockholm double as a bar, so check out the listings in our 'Eat' section as well.

It seems to be a dictum in Sweden that the less drinking there's done during the week, the more excuse there is to go mad at weekends, and the Swedes do this in style. Weekends start on Thursday and the drinking doesn't stop till Monday morning. Alcohol tolerance levels must be among the highest in Europe. 'Drink to get drunk' is the general cry and the bars of Stockholm make the most of their enthusiastic clientele.

Restaurants with bar facilities stay open late throughout the week for those who need a nightcap (or two), and bars at the weekend generally don't close their doors until about 2am. Often places will feature a dance-floor or entirely separate club space downstairs, into which intoxicated revellers can stumble and spend more money on cocktails. Good examples of this are Buddha Bar and Grodan, both of which attract a beautiful, fun-loving and wealthy crowd.

Be prepared to take a well-loaded wallet as drinks do not come cheap. A beer will generally set you back around 45kr, while cocktails begin at 90kr. The cocktails are well worth it, and the range of exotic concoctions is never-ending.

The story is that a cocktail menu acts more as an 'inspiration list' than anything else. If you have a favourite weird and wonderful invention, most barmen will be only too happy to have a go at mixing it, or suggest a similar alternative.

Aside from cocktails, the Swedes know their wine and you'll find extensive lists in most restaurants and bars. Places such as Operakällaren and Divino have a choice so varied you'll be studying it for a while, but with their own well-stocked cellars they are on hand and in the know to offer you some help.

With most bars in Stockholm attached to restaurants, bar snacks are of a high standard in many places. There are few bars that do not have their own separate and often much more reasonably priced menu, where a salad or sandwich will fill a gap. In some cases, these snacks might be preferable to the restaurant alternative. For example, Pontus in the Greenhouse's warm and friendly bar offers a cheaper choice of food in less formal surroundings than the opulent upstairs section.

The bars here are as different as the drinks, and you won't be short of interesting and diversely populated venues. Try the Lydmar for the music crowd or Operabaren for something more sedate. Whoever you are and whatever your preferences, there will be something here to suit you.

Anna Khan, Riddargatan 12, Östermalm.
Tel: 440 30 00 www.annakhan.com
Open: 5pm–1am. Closed Sunday.

Not strictly Indian, its style has definite shades of Southern Asia in both design and its imaginative drinks list. Stureplan regulars have fallen on Anna Khan since its recent opening, stirred by the prospect of an ambitious, Bombay-inspired eatery, which melds beautifully with its equally hip neighbours. As a result, the customers are all passionate about food and life. The place buzzes with frenetic conversation amid soulful music, and as the evening progresses the foodies spill over from the restaurant to the modern-looking bar and lounge. Khan, the owner, has found a

way of making her own name a primary feature, with haphazard As and Ks creating a logo on under-lit dark wood. The lounge is more about comfort and crams bright silks and sequinned cushions onto narrow banquettes. The warmth, excitement and colour of Eastern life shines through, but without the kitsch of so many places that try to blend these influences with those of the West.

Anno 1647, Peder Myndes Backe 5, Slussen, Södermalm.
Tel: 442 16 95 www.anno1647.se
Open: 5pm–midnight Monday–Thursday;
4pm–1am Friday–Saturday.

Slussen is an odd part of town, stuck half-way between Södermalm and Gamla Stan in a kind of no-man's-land. Hotel,

restaurant and bar, Anno 1647 is situated in the middle of Slussen, and reflects this in its resonance of both the Old Town and the more distinctive characteristics of south Stockholm. Blending traditional flower-filled windowsills with an arty atmosphere created by an abstract film projected on a wall covered with disproportionately drawn figures, the bar is a comforting mish-mash of familiar and unusual design. Peer out of frosty windows at the street above and feel safely hidden away in this cavern-like room. It's ideal for a late afternoon pick-me-up after wandering around the ever-entertaining streets of either Gamla Stan or Södermalm, or for an early evening drink before you head off for dinner in either direction. All sorts gather here for exactly this reason and, stepping outside, the views of Gondolen suspended above the lights reflected in the water are stunning.

Aubergine, Linnégatan 38, Östermalm.
Tel: 660 02 04 www.aubergine.se
Open: 11.30am–midnight Monday–Thursday;
11.30am–1am Friday–Saturday.

Despite the name, this restaurant's association with the aubergine is a mystery – aside from a trophy model of the purple vegetable at the bar, it seems in no way to have influenced

103

either the décor or the food. However, it is perhaps a duly chic title for the location and hip interior, both of which entice a primarily local crowd for pre- and post-dinner drinks and more occasionally for the French/Swedish food. You are, as ever, spoilt for choice wandering along Jungsgatan, since with Zoe (see page 98) next door and Halv Grek Plus Turk (see page 81) not much further on, you could indulge almost any culinary or alcoholic penchant. Located in the centre of it all, Aubergine's intimate ambience is ideal for close encounters or hushed conversation over a lingering drink. Although it is distinctively decorated with amorphous ironwork attached to the ends of semi-circular iron rails, it remains embracingly warm; indeed, its atmosphere extends to the restaurant, where you might be tempted to seek out that elusive aubergine while sampling the impressive wine list.

Berns Vinbar, Berzelii Park, Box 16340, Norrmalm.
Tel: 566 325 23 www.berns.se
Open: 11.30am–3pm, 5pm–1am daily

The Vinbar has just taken on a whole new lease of life, originally a dark and smoky room just off the main dining room, it has spread into the glamour of the restaurant. In its new incarnation it has combined with a seafood bar to become a sophisticated place to enjoy a quiet drink with an excellent glass of wine. The waiters are all trained sommeliers who choose the wines themselves and the menu changes weekly. The choice of wines is exquisite, drawn from both the Old and New World and presented at a perfect time for drinking. It is a pleasure to drink here as the staff are unbelievably knowledgeable and good wine is treated with the deference it deserves. Even though it is so close to the nightclubs the Vinbar is perfect to come to for a more relaxed drink, hence the sophisticated company that you'll inevitably keep. Cocktails are available as usual on request if a glass of wine doesn't meet your needs.

Brasserie Godot, Grev Turegatan 36, Östermalm.
Tel: 660 06 14 www.godot.se
Open: 5pm–1am. Closed Sunday.

The cocktail list in this predominantly white bar/brasserie attracts the Östermalm 20-somethings in their hundreds. The brasserie is partly sectioned off from the drinking side of things and, although it serves high-quality *steak frites*, it is left in the shade when compared with the creations lighting up next door. With blazers and chinos aplenty, crowds fall on Godot for this sole reason, which poses a problem to nearby new openers such as Hotellet (see page 110) whose standards, although high, will be hard-pushed to steal the prized reputation of its neighbouring competitor. Such status is achieved, it seems, in the joys of a list so long that it is impossible to improve on any concoction with your own unique additions. In a town where the bar staff can make most drinks to order, cocktail lists this spectacular are a novelty. The choices range from modern variations on old favourites (five different Bloody Marys) to the frankly bizarre. The common denominator is the skill and ease with which all the drinks are mixed.

Buddha Bar, Biblioteksgatan 9, Östermalm.
Tel: 545 185 00 www.buddha.se
Open: 11.30am–12am Monday–Tuesday; 11.30am–3am
Wednesday–Thursday; 11.30am–4am Friday; 1pm–4am Saturday.

The name should be familiar and Buddha Bar, Stockholm, is doing its best to keep up with the Paris original. Some are disappointed by a bar that, in a town of exciting new design concepts, is simply a copy of a bigger and better version. The crowds that gather here on Saturday nights, however, might beg to differ. Unsurprising but entertaining décor consists of numerous Buddha statuettes glowing in alcoves in the red walls. An opulent colour scheme sets the tone for indulgence as hard-hitting beats fill both levels of the bar late into the evening. Controversy over Buddha's popularity is dissipated in the light of the groups that habitually appear here. This consists not only of Östermalm regulars, who drop in for a drink on passing, but also those who have had to travel in from further afield to enjoy the bar's ambience. The crowd is mixed as a result and the different groups eventually separate off to their preferred clubs once the vibe dies down.

East, Stureplan 13, Östermalm.
Tel: 611 49 59 www.east.se
Open: 11.30am–3am Monday–Friday; 5pm–3am Saturday–Sunday.

As one of Östermalm's most popular sushi joints during the day, East attracts a crowd that is typical of this area. However, the dynamic of East is turned upside-down in the evening, thanks to a much more diverse mix of people. The reasons for such a significant change are found in the pounding rhythms, toxic cocktails and funky décor, all of which bring in hip-hop lovers from all

corners of the city. From 6pm, the long bar is packed out to suffocation point, with hidden booths illuminated dimly by under-lit photographs of beautiful people in exotic locations. This place is more about 'cool' than beauty, however, and the bouncers outside are more than aware of this. To glide in effortlessly, dress up in your funkiest threads and be there by 10.30pm. Open until 3am every single day of the week, in terms of atmosphere and location it's ideal for late drinks, a brief boogie, or just as a starting point for a long night ahead. East's success lies in its location on the corner of Stureplan, the biggest meeting-point in central Stockholm and at weekends the place from which the hordes disperse to one of the many clubs in the vicinity.

Grodan, Grev Turegatan 16, Östermalm.
Tel: 679 61 00 www.grodan.nu
Open: 11.30am–1am Monday–Thursday; 11.30am–3am Friday; noon–2am Saturday.

Grodan must be Stockholm's most consistently fashionable hangout. It has sat in its prime location for years and its regulars cling to it while introducing selected newcomers to its many charms. Amonge these are a great restaurant and an even better club

(see page 136), but the bar area is where the Östermalm hordes collect. This is standing-room only unless you turn up very early, but jostling with the attractive crowd to fight your way to the bar is all part of the fun. Wait your turn to be served by a deliciously competent barman who'll ask what you want without offering a menu. This is Stockholm at its most typical – invent your own wild cocktail and you'll be given something as close to your dream drink as the barman can make it. The décor comes in a bizarre mix of styles. If you walk through to the restaurant you'll find yourself in Renaissance territory, which is in stark contrast to the abstractly modern bar. Here, life-size photos of half-naked models are totally in keeping with the beautiful clientele.

Halv Trappa Plus Gard, Lästmakargatan 3, Östermalm.
Tel: 678 10 50 www.halvtrappaplusgard.se
Open: 5pm–1am Tuesday–Thursday; 5pm–3am Friday–Saturday.

Full of trendy professionals, some of whom have had dinner in the Oriental-styled restaurant below, the bar can best be described as 1970s avant-garde – orange plastic chairs are juxtaposed with Chinese lanterns, resulting in an unusual but fashionable fusion of tastes. The bar is independent of the restaurant and has its own entrance; a chance encounter with an awkward bouncer may mean that you have to eat downstairs first, before you can sneak up to avoid any difficulties outside. Inside it's

packed to the brim with music and media darlings whose conversation over a mix of hip-hop and soul will consist largely of who signed who, who's going up in the world and who's past it. If this banter doesn't appeal to you, you won't feel out of place kicking back in one of the two lounges to observe the media whores in their natural habitat. In summer the mood is more relaxed, the backyard terrace is opened and a similar rabble warm their hands under heaters – they take themselves less seriously without the backdrop of pretentious minimalist interior design. On a balmy August evening, Halv Trappa Plus Gard is a definite Stureplan favourite.

Hotellet, Linnégatan 18, Östermalm.
Tel: 442 89 00 www.hotellet.se
Open: 4pm–1am Monday–Thursday; 4pm–3am Friday–Saturday.

Very new and still seeking widespread approval, Hotellet should gain deserved support from the regulars frequenting the many bars and restaurants in the area. It's up against some tough competition, including Aubergine and Elverket, but with a well-marketed restaurant, great location and plenty of space for big parties, the chic ambience should hold its own. This is especially true with regard to the large back garden where one of the two Hotellet bars serves up a great daiquiri for you to sip while you recline on a retro *chaise longue*. Hotellet's space is a real advantage, particularly during colder periods when the long bar in its rusty orange colours and warm wooden furnishings comes into its own. There are plans to open a club beneath the bar where the room is equally expansive and this, given the present popularity of Hotellet's bars on a Friday night, should keep the

punters in rather than drifting off to Kharma (see page 157) or
Sture Compagniet (see page 165). It needs this extra dimension,
as novelty and excellent cocktails have attracted a chic crowd so
far, but the reputation of Brasserie Godot next door is one that
Hotellet might struggle to better.

Ice Bar, Nordic Sea Hotel, Vasaplan, Box 884, Norrmalm.
Tel: 505 630 00 www.nordichotels.se
Open: 4.30pm–midnight Monday–Friday; 3pm–midnight Saturday.

You might have heard of Sweden's Ice Hotel; this is just a taste of
what you will experience there. Situated in the lobby of the
Nordic Sea (see page 45), the Ice Bar is the hotel's pride and joy
and, unsurprisingly, draws in the odd tourist. Conditions of –5°C
might not be everyone's idea of fun, but it certainly makes a
change from the average watering-hole. Fur-lined coats and

warm boots are provided for customers before they venture in
to sample the only alcohol available – vodka. This is served in ice
glasses, which is appropriate given that the rest of the bar and
room are also made of ice. The ice is imported from the north
of Sweden and comes from the same source as that of the Ice
Hotel. This is worth a visit for novelty factor more than real
enjoyment of a drink, but it's amusing enough for as many minutes as you can bear the cold.

Isole, Biblioteksgatan 5, Östermalm.
Tel: 611 84 08 www.isole.se
Open: 11.30am–2pm, 5pm–1am (3am at weekends)

Yet another of the many restaurant/bar/clubs, this is more of a place to drink and dance. The drinking is the bigger feature, however, and will undoubtedly affect how much is done of the latter, as there is no formal dance-floor. If it's a glass of wine you're after on your way to a nearby restaurant, then stick with the

more sedate bar as you enter Isole, but for more frenzied evenings, head immediately downstairs. A red glow radiates outwards from strips and squares of light on the white walls, creating an environment that attracts the über-cool who have quickly discovered it since its recent opening. Isole replaced what was Sophie's – an Östermalm haunt that successfully rolled along for years, and had a firmly established reputation to live up to. There shouldn't be a problem, however – manager Joachim also owns Södermalm's very lucrative Metro, which gives Isole the double advantage of filling newcomers with a sense of familiarity and confidence and bringing to Östermalm a slice of unique character from the south, both in terms of attitude and music. This lot won't be on their feet until much later in the evening, but instead prefer to chill out on red leather banquettes engaging in philosophical conversation. We were assured of no '19-year-old brats' (admittedly a common feature in this part of Östermalm), but instead a collection of deep thinkers who are seriously into their music, in this case hip-hop and drum'n'bass.

Lokal, Scheelegatan 8, Kungsholmen.
Tel: 650 98 09
Open: 4pm–1am Sunday–Thursday; 4pm–2am Friday–Saturday.

Lokal perfectly suits its name since, situated on Kungsholmen, a more residential than happening island, it brings in a regular clientele of locals who come back because they rate it. And it's

not because Kungsholmen is so lacking in decent places to get a drink that everyone in the vicinity flocks here in desperation. Indeed, Lokal is the first of a group of bars that are putting this island back on the style map. Although it doubles as a good restaurant, the food alone is not a good enough reason to venture out of known haunts to these less recognizable streets, but the bar and lounge areas most certainly are. Sporting a white interior with a contrasting slash of deep red wall overlooking the lounge section, Lokal emits an inviting and irresistible glow which will lure you in if you wander past in search of other Scheelegatan treasures. The bar stretches around most of the room, martinis are served in a myriad versions and the DJ lifts the mood from soulful to a more energizing vibe mid-evening. Drinks are served until 3am and you will find yourself unwilling to move once the place fills up, since it has such a mixed and cool clientele.

Lydmar Hotel Bar, Sturegatan 10, Östermalm.
Tel: 566 113 00 www.lydmar.se
Open: 11.30am–1am Sunday–Thurs; noon–2am Saturday.

Stockholm has quickly caught on to the hotel-bar phenomenon, and located amongst the chic bars and restaurants of Östermalm, the Lydmar has made it its most obvious feature. It stands apart from the others in its graft of musical influences – black and white photographs of gospel singers watch over the new breed of jazz, funk and soul singers who regularly perform live. The Lydmar looks like a modern take on a jazz lounge, with long black leather sofas lining the walls and elegant chandeliers hang-

ing from beams just outside. The clientele are as decadent as the interior: a funky crowd sips cocktails and chills to the music. During the day the bar can seem a little stark and somewhat depressing, but as the sun goes down the beautiful people come out to play.

Mården, Tulegatan 24, Vasastan.
Tel: 612 65 50 www.marden.se
Open: 5pm–midnight Tuesday–Wednesday;
5pm–1am Thursday–Saturday.

With a drinks list promising every cocktail under the sun,

Mården's bar is an attractive proposition. Minutes from Storstad and Olssons Skor, it is most popular for evening drinks at weekends, before the 'in' crowd move on to dance. Soulful music and a spot-lit white room make for a chilled out and trendy atmosphere. Projections of grungy models or nameless cities cloak the walls, along with arty framed photographs. Surprisingly, however, the atmosphere and service are unpretentious; previously an

apoteket (chemist), the place is named after the pharmacy's traditionally assigned animal – in this case, a ferret – and maintains a down-to-earth mood. Black leather on dark wood is the look adopted for the bar furniture while the adjoining restaurant contrasts with citrus motifs. If too many daiquiris have reduced you to a level where you are unable to walk further through Vasastan to find dinner, Mården's continental cuisine is delicious.

Markattan, Stora Nygatan 41, Gamla Stan.
Tel: 440 09 19 www.markattan.com
Open: 5pm–midnight Tuesday–Thursday; 5pm–3am
Friday–Saturday.

Decent bars in Gamla Stan – at least those that are not full to bursting with sightseers – are few and far between. The two most attractive have opened only recently, and are on the same street only yards away from each other. Unlike the stark Mistral (see below), Markattan consists of a maze of cavernous tunnels, lit predominantly by the soft glow of candlelight. Further warmth is added by the plethora of red furniture; different den-like rooms hold anything from comfy high-backed chairs to wooden dining tables for Markattan's European cuisine. From 11pm onwards, however, these old cellar vaults become one big party, especially at weekends. The din from this basement venue pours out onto Stora Nyagatan to tempt passers-by. A great atmosphere is created when the DJ kicks in to step up the mood, and Stockholm's grander locals dance the night away in underground style.

Mistral, Lilla Nygatan 26, Gamla Stan.
Open: 5pm–1am Sunday–Thursday; 5pm–3am Friday–Saturday.

The second of Gamla Stan's new up-and-coming bars, Mistral is not far from its partner in crime, Markattan. Dissimilar in every sense, however, it is tiny and very white, which is unusual given the need for almost every other establishment in the Old Town to fill its rooms with brightly coloured tablecloths, clichéd Swedish souvenirs and a faux rustic décor. A room verging on austere is saved by abstract art and piles of cushions. Mind you, any room in Gamla Stan can be homely simply because of its location among the winding cobbled streets and small terracotta-painted houses. Despite its short history Mistral has already made its name with its special drinks, which include different types of beer infused with herbs. The beer is definitely

worth a try and is delicious if your taste runs to the unusual.
An equally white restaurant of the same name is next door, but
save your appetite for superior local restaurants such as Grill
Ruby (see page 78) and Bistro Ruby (see page 63). Then pop
back to Mistral for a few late-night drinks and a true taste of
Stockholm life, since this is one of the few bars in the Old Town
that is not frequented by hordes of camera-clutching holiday-
makers.

Niva, Sveavägen 53, Vasastan.
Open: 11.30am–midnight Sunday–Thursday;
11.30am–1am Friday–Saturday.

Niva is improbably located in the less happening, business district
of Vasastan, but don't be put off by the slightly dilapidated shops
and cafés surrounding it, since you'll be heading here on one
mission in particular. Whatever your sport of choice, there is
every likelihood that that all-important match will be showing on
the huge screen which dominates the middle of the bar. As at
the Tudor Arms, Premiership matches are aired at weekends and
any other games of note throughout the week. Preferable to the
smoky atmosphere of the Grevgatan Pub, here it's fresher and
less tourist-oriented, and rival supporters are at their friendliest.
Filling snacks are available through the day, and the more exclusive bars and restaurants are only a few minutes' walk back on
Kungsgatan, which leads down to Stureplan. A good environment

for a drink and some football on a Sunday afternoon, Niva is only slightly let down by its dubious surroundings.

Operabaren, Operahuset, Karl XII's torg, Norrmalm.
Tel: 676 58 00 www.operakallaren.se
Open 11.30am–1am Monday–Wednesday;
11.30am–2am Thursday–Friday; 1pm–2am Saturday.

Although Operabaren and the nearby O Baren are easily confused, the two are poles apart in terms of mood and style. The Jugendstil décor in this old-fashioned room provides a club setting for reading newspapers in deep dark-brown leather armchairs, or for a nightcap in ultra-civilized surroundings, until the bar closes at 2am. It's just in front of the relaxed Bakfickan and through from the raucous Café Opera and the justifiably

extortionate Operakällaren next door, so if you're in this part of town you might find its more sober atmosphere preferable for a quiet conversation, or just a more affordable option for a drink or bar dinner. The old waiters in white starched jackets know their wine lists by heart. Don't be put off by its resemblance to a traditional gentlemen's club, but appreciate the classic surroundings — very Swedish with colonial touches — and the view over the greenery of Kungsträdgården and beyond to the shimmering waterfront.

Sky Bar, Radisson SAS Viking Hotel, Vasagatan 1, Norrmalm.
Tel: 506 540 00 www.radisson.com
Open: 6–10pm daily

This is the Radisson Viking's most unique feature. It is situated on the top floor, and its view is its selling-point: floor-to-ceiling windows offer a panoramic outlook across most of Stockholm. The bar is popular not only with hotel guests but also with Swedish businessmen introducing Stockholm to clients, or couples seeking a spectacular setting for an intimate drink. Thanks to its position in the middle of the financial district of Norrmalm, the high-class restaurants of Östermalm and Vasastan are close by, so that you can enjoy Sky Bar for its penthouse perspective and then leave the Viking for better dinner prospects.

Tuesdays, Thursdays and Sundays are, somewhat unusually, Soap Bar's biggest nights, and this is down to its clientele. The reason for this is that the bar sits less than a minute's walk from Dramatiska Teatern, where performances towards the beginning and end of the week are the most popular. The pre- and more often post-theatre crowd pours into Soap Bar from 10.30pm to discuss the evening's dramatics in a down-to-earth environment. The place thus provides a rare opportunity, in a city where the weekends are mad and the weekdays mostly quiet, to go to a bar

with a fully charged atmosphere midweek. Consisting of crowds of regulars and those purely in town for the theatre, an exceptionally diverse rabble packs out the tiny bar space. The restaurant darlings are out in force on a Tuesday while Sunday evenings here offer an opportunity to banish those end-of-weekend blues. Whoever you are and whenever you go, Soap Bar is never boring. The bar staff know everyone in the place, and most of the drinkers appear to be their closest friends, so go prepared to be drawn in by the friendly atmosphere and watch the barmen enthusiastically try to make your favourite cocktail.

Storstad, Döbelnsgatan 44, Vasastan.
Tel: 673 38 00 www.storstad.se
Open: 3pm–1am Sunday–Wednesday;
3pm–3am Thursday–Saturday.

It seems unfair that despite Storstad's great European food, it has been increasingly labelled as a watering-hole rather than a restaurant. However, people have continued to gather at this bar over many years – indeed, so much so that the idea had to be extended next door (see Olssons Skor, page 163) – thus testifying to the fact that it is one of the coolest bars in this part of Vasastan. With its dark wood, brown leather and creamy interior, it has a clean and sophisticated look. On weekdays the post-work suits who frequent the bar only serve to reinforce this impression. As the week progresses, expect more variety as the alternative Södermalm crowd and Stureplan's *fashionistas* venture further from home for an interesting night on the town. The long room becomes packed and tends to overflow to the upstairs bar, which, with its red-draped surroundings, is more sinful than pure. Although it's in style all year round, a summer's evening inevitably brings in the most enviable beauties as the warm weather provides an opportunity to drink outside. Here the crowds from Storstad and Olssons Skor merge, creating an interesting and individual throng.

Tranan, Karlbergsvägen 14, Vasastan.
Tel: 527 281 00 www.sturehof.com
Open: 11.30am–1am Monday–Friday; 5pm–1am Saturday–Sunday.

Tranan's restaurant clientele is described by regulars as the per-
sonification of classic Swedish social life, and the downstairs bar
upholds its reputation as a quintessential Stockholm watering-

hole. The cellar-like basement manages to elude any suggestion
of dinginess, remaining warm and full of life on almost any day of
the week. It's also down-to-earth, from the simple wood and
brown leather interior to the cocktail menu written in chalk on
a blackboard above the bar. Its lack of pretentiousness also
applies to the group who drink here, who consist largely of
those who have eaten upstairs and whose legs, after several large
glasses of wine, won't carry them to nearby Storstad or Mården.
So if you trip down the stairs to this less obviously hip but in
fact equally cool spot you're promised a lazy but fun-loving
evening. Others will travel quite a distance for the delights of
Tranan's unaffected environment, among them many professionals
who drop in for a pick-me-up after meetings in surrounding
Vasastan. Later in the evening the crowd becomes more lively,
the music begins to pump and the alcohol flows. There will be
few surprises in terms of redecoration or change of vibe: this
has been here for years and its popularity will ensure it continues in the same vein for some time to come.

Tudor Arms, Grevgatan 31, Östermalm.

Tel: 660 27 12

Open: 11.30am–11pm Monday–Friday; 2–11pm Saturday; 2–7pm Sunday.

Without a doubt the most English pub in Stockholm, so your reasons for coming here should either involve a homesick craving for bitter, or a particularly critical football match. Don't expect anything even verging on Scandinavian culture. Bar staff are English, and the typical pub menu features scampi and fish

and chips – but much better than you'll find at home! Along with the typical pub grub, there won't be any disappointments with the drinks, either. Everything from Tennants to Guinness is available, so most tastes are catered for. Collapse with your pint onto the Tudor-style furniture, with dark wooden beams overhead, and prepare for the big game. Most matches are aired – the Premiership at weekends and other matches when necessary. You needn't worry about the lack of big game atmosphere either, since with other like-minded tourists and ex-pats, you will quickly feel very much at home surrounded by the traditional participative bellowing at the on-screen action.

Undici, Sturegatan 22, Östermalm.

Tel: 661 66 17 www.undici.se

Open: 5pm–1am Tuesday–Thursday; 5pm–3am Friday–Saturday.

Yet another of Stockholm's celebrity-run joints, Undici ('eleven' in Italian) refers to the number on the back of owner and ex-footballer Tomas Brolin's shirt. This in itself brings in the local celebrities but it is recommended more for its bar than its adjoining restaurant. There are two reasons for this, first that on Friday and Saturday nights Undici opens until 3am, and secondly because if you're really after luxurious Italian food, you won't pay much more for a far higher standard up the road in Divino (see page 67). The late-night opening is almost made obsolete by the presence of Kharma, Sture Compagniet, Laroy *et al.*, 100 metres down from here, but Undici gathers a great pre-clubbing crowd who are up for an eventful night ahead. It does make for interesting people-watching and early interaction with fellow Spy Bar fans (**see page 164**). Bare interiors are livened up by the sheer quantity of people, as well as by a bar lit with colours reminiscent of all things Italian. You shouldn't have too many problems getting in; atmosphere, it's better to arrive here later rather than earlier.

Updates and notes...

snack...

Sweden's climate encourages the café culture trend in Stockholm where establishments metamorphose from summer to winter incarnations. From mid-October to mid-April Swedish laws prohibit tables being put outside cafés and restaurants. This may seem extreme, but – as common sense dictates – it is simply too cold to sit in the open air.

Consequently, during the winter, many cafés function as informal restaurants rather than coffee houses, and this is especially apparent in the food and drink they choose to serve. There are, of course, the standard establishments that specialize in a cappuccino and slice of cake, but these are less common than those whose menus stretch to three-course meals.

Expect standard Caesar salads, *croque monsieur*s and BLTs, but also imaginative ranges of pasta-, fish- and meat-based dishes. In winter Stockholm professionals begin to fill such places as Crème from 11.30am onwards, not for a quick espresso, but for a more substantial meal to get them through the frozen afternoon.

The boundaries between restaurants and cafés are, for this reason, difficult to define. Cafés really come into their own during the summer, when tables are spread out on cobbled squares in Gamla Stan, and Stureplan is packed with a self-confident designer-clad crowd watching the elegant passers-by. For those chillier days when everyone wraps up to sit over steaming cups of coffee, blankets are hung by café staff over the backs of steel chairs.

Those with a sweeter tooth needn't despair: although Stockholm cafés excel at savoury dishes, every place has a counter brimming with sugary goodies. The typical treat is sticky fruit tart, usually blueberry, as well as huge muffins and rich chocolate cake. For more traditional Swedish delicacies, head to Vette Katten. All this is sure to recharge the batteries mid-sightseeing, and there are plenty of inviting places whichever part of town you're in.

Give both types of café a try. Calle P, with its odd but delicious fusion of Asian and Italian snacks, is perfect for a lunch that is more sustaining than a solitary sandwich. Baresso, on the other hand, is the place to take your early morning newspaper for a quiet read over a coffee, while the world passes by.

7 Knop, Skånegatan 87, Södermalm.
Tel: 642 06 04
Open: 10am–9pm daily

Among the alternative establishments of Skånegatan nestles
7 Knop, which is decidely conventional in comparison with the
yoga studios, juice bars and second-hand clothes shops nearby.
Touches of south Stockholm's rejection of all things establishment are present, as well as the clientele, most of whom sit back
on cushions with their feet up on the nearest available chair. Set
down from the street, the interior is nautical in design: whitewashed walls and large white cushions embellish simple benches
furnished with blue striped cushions. Any noble intention to sample only an organic smoothie is soon forgotten when the tempting tit-bits on the counter catch your eye. The mood is so chilled

that you can easily while away a couple of hours here listening to
a little soul or funk, whether you eat or not. 7 Knop stays open
late into the evening but the café atmosphere lingers, so unless
you have a night-time craving for a slice of chocolate cake it
would be more sensible to use this as a strictly daytime hangout.

Baresso, Nybrogatan 21, Östermalm.
Tel: 661 86 61 www.baresso.se
Open: 8am–8pm Monday–Friday; 8am–6pm Saturday;
9am–6pm Sunday.

Close to Crème and seemingly more popular, packing the same amount of people into a smaller space. Baresso is less cool in terms of musical ambience, but more focused on the array of rich chocolate muffins and fruit tarts which litter the counter. This, unlike some of the others mentioned in this section, is a café in the usual sense of the word. Blackboards detail assorted cakes, new coffee varieties and many of the more substantial savoury dishes, which are specialities of the café culture in Stockholm. Perfectly located either for an early morning scan of the papers or for resting tired feet after a long afternoon, this café provides good coffee while you relax and watch the world go by.

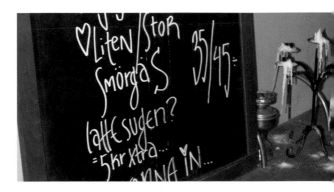

Bonan, Humlegardsgatan 9, Östermalm.
Open: 8am–7pm Monday–Friday; 10am–7pm Saturday;
11am–7pm Sunday.

Dimly lit and filled with dark wooden tables and chairs, this is a winter place. Retreat in here for a hot drink and a sweet pastry – with its great location in the middle of Östermalm's hustle and bustle, you are bound to come across it. The subdued lighting is very seductive, and enhances the huge coffee beans painted on the walls next to shady stick figures, who jump out of the shadows. Customers sit huddled in warm clothes, hands wrapped round comfortingly large mugs. Perfect for intimate conversation, this spot is a retreat from the noisy streets outside. Having escaped the madness, you won't want to leave this little haven of calm, but then again all the benefits of Östermalm are just round the corner.

Café Albert, Birger Jarlsgatan 5, Östermalm.
Open: 8am–midnight Monday–Thursday;
8am–2am Friday–Saturday; 9am–11pm Sunday.

Many of Stockholm's cafés have unusually late opening hours, but this place is in a league of its own. A café in the true sense of the word, serving coffee, cake and not much else, it nevertheless attracts a young post-clubbing crowd at the weekends. Food is served almost until closing and chairs with blankets strewn across them are placed outside, so that customers spill out onto the street late into the night. The café is a hub of activity at this

time, tempting in passers-by with promises of a better class of snack than the nearby Burger King. Older party-goers may feel a little out of place, and don't expect a quiet cup of coffee whatever the time of day. Groups of friends meet here to shout their night's gossip to each other, and they don't mind who hears it.

Café Entré, Nordiska Kompaniet, Hamngatan 18–20, Norrmalm.
Tel: 762 87 11
Open: 10am–7pm Monday–Friday; 10am–6pm Saturday; 12–5pm Sunday.

The urge to flop down in Café Entré after a heavy afternoon's shopping in Stockholm's most deluxe department store is almost irresistible. Situated on the ground floor of NK, it is cleverly positioned to catch the big spenders before they leave. Groups of friends meet to gossip over the wide selection of sandwiches and salads before deciding which boutique to visit next. The

unexciting décor, comfortable but dreary banquettes and wooden tables and chairs are mostly hidden by the day's shopping – huge Dolce & Gabbana bags littering the seats, clutched by well-groomed purchasers, make for far more interesting viewing than the actual interior. That said, the café looks up into the store's elegant atrium, where the hustle and bustle of sales on all floors can be observed in full swing.

Café Momba, Norrmalmstorg, Norrmalm.
Tel: 678 72 72
Open: 9am–11pm Sunday–Friday; 9am–2am Saturday.

Aside from the weekend nightclub, Momba operates – as its name suggests – as a café during the day, and it's first-rate. Its location in the middle of Norrmalmstorg, within yards of NK, PK Huset and countless designer boutiques, makes for riveting people-watching over a plate of pasta, a huge *ciabatta* sandwich,

or one of an endless array of salads. During the summer, sit in the open air or under the marquee that converts to the night-club at weekends. If it's too cold, you can take refuge within Momba's intriguing structure: built up on stilts, it provides a fascinating 'goldfish bowl' effect because of its octagonal shape. A bar dominates the upstairs room, around which cushioned banquettes rest against the glass, affording a comfortable space to view outside goings-on. You'll find English newspapers available in the little newsagent below, which is part of the café, although if you're planning to catch up with the news over lunch, expect papers to be a day behind.

Calle P, Berzelii Park, Östermalm.
Tel: 566 325 15 www.berns.se
Open: 9am–midnight Sunday–Friday; 9am–1am Saturday.

Another section of the seemingly never-ending Berns, this sits in the square that the bar and most of the hotel rooms overlook. You can expect simpler fare here than in the restaurant, although

it is in no way inferior in quality. Berns maintains its standards whether it's at its most informal or executing its grandest ventures. The square is filled with tables and chairs during the summer, while the glass building's interior of stripy cushioned benches and long wooden tables creates a natural environment all year round. The menu comprises a bizarre blend of Asian and Italian cuisine, so that you can tuck into a huge bowl of Tom Kha Gai soup, or a toasted focaccia filled with mozzarella, parma ham or roasted vegetables; all are mouth-wateringly good. A long list of pizzas is also on standby in case nothing else takes your fancy, but try branching out into less familiar Thai territory, where you will be pleasantly surprised. Since it's open late, drinks here might be a good idea before braving Berns' bar or club.

Coco and Carmen, Banérgatan 7, Östermalm.
Tel: 660 11 05
Open: 11.30am–3pm, 5.30–11pm daily

Owned by eccentric couple Coco and Carmen Frisk, this classy café is full of delicious surprises. With specialities that include home-made barley water for a refreshing break on a hot

summer's day, this is a breezy and relaxed establishment. Just round the corner are the lush gardens of Djurgården, and with it the fantastic Vasa and Nordic museums. After a leisurely stroll around these in the morning, Coco and Carmen is the perfect stop for lunch. Fantastic eggs Benedict make a wonderful light meal, while the fish of the day, cooked however Coco has decreed that morning, will fill a larger hole. This is one of the cafés that could be labelled either café or restaurant, since it opens for dinner too. However, with such an abundance of exciting restaurants in Stockholm, leave this coolly decorated spot for a lunchtime rendezvous.

Crème, Nybrogatan 16, Östermalm.
Tel: 660 77 70 www.creme.nu
Open: 8am–10pm Monday–Friday; 10am–7pm Saturday; 11am–7pm Sunday.

Minutes from Saluhallen (the covered market), fashionable Birger Jarlsgatan and the media companies of Sturegatan, Crème attracts early morning professionals needing a caffeine fix, and a flow of solitary newspaper readers or small groups of locals during the rest of the day. The coffee itself is excellent and may be the best reason for dropping in, since with such treasures as Lisa Elmqvist 2 minutes up the road, it is not worth having an average bowl of fish soup here when the real McCoy is so close by. Crème, although essentially a café like Baresso, is more stylish, with beige minimalist décor and displays of abstract art. Its

soundtrack of hip-hop beats adds an injection of youth without
intruding upon conversation. This is one of the many places in
Stockholm that it just makes sense to stop at, whether you're on
your way up to the food market or down to the waterfront; and
its exterior is inviting enough to convince you that you need a
cup of coffee whatever the time of day.

Divino, Karlavägen 28, Norrmalm.
Tel: 611 02 99 www.divino.se
Open: 9am–7pm Monday–Friday; 11am–5pm Saturday–Sunday.

Divino's reputation as the Italian restaurant for the self-indulgent
does wonders for its next door deli/café. The making of
extremely strong Italian coffee is taken very seriously by the
exuberant owner, who swears you won't find better in

Stockholm. Sit inside among the endless bottles of olive oil, truffles, etc., while the smells of the freshest cheeses and salamis waft over you, or outside, taking in the sights and sounds of Karlavagen, one of Ostermalm's busiest streets. This is not so much a cosy café as the place where you go for the pure appreciation of excellent coffee and luxurious Italian foods. You'll be pushed to walk out of here without buying something you never knew you wanted.

Elt Litet Hak, Grev Turegatan 15, Östermalm.
Tel: 660 13 09 www.eltlitethak.se
Open: 11.30am–midnight Monday–Friday;
1pm–midnight Saturday; 5–11pm Sunday.

Anyone with a café/bar opposite Grodan (see page 108) has a good chance of attracting affluent business, if only from its overflow. Nevertheless, Elt Litet Hak – literally 'A Small Spot' – stands on its own reputation. Serving considerably more traditional Swedish fare than much of this café-packed pedestrian street, it offers a haven of warmth and comfort, with seafood casseroles crammed with squid and shrimps. The upstairs space contains deep sofas on which to lounge about and observe the goings-on downstairs. This is most appropriate for the winter time, but in the summer plenty of steel tables outside lure in the chic crowd typical of this area. By and large a haunt for the young, it fills up

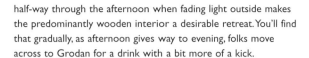

half-way through the afternoon when fading light outside makes the predominantly wooden interior a desirable retreat. You'll find that gradually, as afternoon gives way to evening, folks move across to Grodan for a drink with a bit more of a kick.

Foam, Karlavägen 75, Östermalm.
Tel: 600 09 96 www.cafefoam.com
Open: 10am–9pm Monday–Friday; noon–9pm Saturday–Sunday.

Foam is home to a mass of beautiful young things: pretty 15- to

25-year-olds float in and out of this bright Valhallavägen spot, which is probably more appealing to gregarious groups than to the solitary customer. Because of its central location, you could stop here *en route* to almost anywhere, whether it's a lunchtime sandwich you're after or an afternoon coffee. Surprisingly, however, given its position, Valhallavägen is less frequented by sightseers than the streets around Stureplan, so it is usually full of Swedish regulars rather than tourists needing to recharge the batteries. You'll find groups of friends draping themselves over the pink, red and lime-green foam sofas, and the 20-something creatives hang their pop art on the walls in the hope it'll be noticed and bought by a passer-by. Light and airy, this is a pleasant little café in which to have a cup of hot chocolate.

Lasse I Parken, Högalidsgatan 56, Långholmen.
Tel: 658 33 95
Open: Winter: 11am–5pm Saturday–Sunday;
Summer: 11am–4.30pm Tuesday–Saturday.

This really does exist, despite being fairly difficult to locate. Look for the greenest area you can find, having first passed Långholmen (see page 41), and you won't be far off. The little wooden house is situated in a small park that overlooks the gardens of the jail, but

it's not nearly as gloomy as it sounds. On the contrary, given a bright summer's afternoon, Lasse I Parken is the ideal spot to take a trip back in time to a dream childhood, complete with fruit pies and thick cheddar sandwiches, while basking in the warm sun filtering through the foliage. An outside theatre sometimes puts on frivolous but entertaining shows, harking back again to a slightly fairy-tale world. If you're staying at Långholmen, this will prove a wonderful summertime retreat from the starkness of your hotel room. If not, it is worth the short bus journey from the city centre for home-baked bread and delicious cheesecake to be sampled in a delightful landscape setting.

Lisa På Torget, Östermalmstorg, Östermalm.
Tel: 662 33 34
Open: 11.30am–11pm Monday–Friday; 1–11pm Saturday–Sunday.
Closed Sunday in winter.

Sister to the culinary experience that is Lisa Elmqvist, Lisa På Torget sits just outside Saluhallen, in the centre of Östermalmstorg. The size of Lisa 'on the square' disqualifies it as a place for an intimate discussion, but it is nevertheless enjoyable, whether you are indoors on a freezing cold afternoon or warming your hands under heaters outside when it's slightly warmer. Inside, four or five wooden tables, under a low cabin roof, have people sitting almost on top of each other. This space is therefore reserved mostly for bundled-up winter evenings, when having a

drink cheek-to-cheek with your neighbours seems to matter less. According to the Stockholm system, between May and mid-October seats outside are draped with blankets to warm a hungry lunch crowd, who are served similar fare to Lisa Elmqvist, as well as the standard, but delicious, toasted sandwich. Prices reflect a pretty ritzy set of regulars, but Lisa can afford to keep them high as the smart punters just keep on coming.

Petite, Östermalmstorg, Östermalm.
Open: 8am–5.30pm daily

Living up to its name, this must be the tiniest café in Stockholm. Sitting rather forlornly on Östermalmstorg, it is dwarfed by the presence next door of Lisa På Torget and the wonderful Saluhall. It makes you want to take pity on it and go in and the interior does not disappoint. The little hut's very limited space is filled to the brim with pastries, sandwiches and coffee machines behind the tiny counter. Cosy, largely because of its size, Petite makes itself a very warm place to be. With room only for four or five people, come and relax quietly with a paper first thing in the morning, watching the comings and goings in the square as fresh produce is unloaded for the food market opposite.

Rosendals Trädgård, Rosendalsterrassen 12, Djurgården.
Tel: 545 812 70 www.rosendalstradgard.com
Open: 11am–5pm daily. Closed mid-November to mid-January.

Essential for time out in rural surroundings, Rosendals is ideal for those with a sweet tooth: this conservatory café is particularly famous for its cakes and sugary temptations. As well as loads of outdoor space, it also has a shop that sells similar specialities just next door. To maximize your enjoyment, take time out from a stroll through the park to appreciate Rosendals' delicacies while admiring the view over Djurgården. Sit under the umbrellas in the park if you can, but the glass house, complete with chandeliers and elegant furnishings, gives you the view with the added bonus of warmth on colder days. During weekends cars are not allowed to drive through the park, so you can either work up an appetite for the café's renowned fruit pies, or take the bus for an easy ride there.

Soap Bar, Nybrogatan 1, Östermalm.
Tel: 611 00 21 www.soapbar.se
Open: 2pm–midnight Monday; 2pm–3am Tuesday–Sunday.

This popular bar is a great place to recharge one's batteries in the middle of the day. You couldn't wish for a better location, on the edge of Birger Jarlsgatan and looking out onto the waterfront, but with easy access to all the shops and sights. The décor fits the bar mood more than that of a café – it's dark with black leather banquettes that dominate the space. However, the staff are down-to-earth, and this goes for the food, too: simple snacks are served all day long. Enough regulars come in here for the menu to be incredibly flexible – if you fancy a something a little different from what's on offer, efforts will be made to accommodate your choice. Although a calm mood is maintained during the

day, the party atmosphere picks up slowly in the early evening, and soulful background music takes on more of a beat. An easy place to rest tired feet, check the map or just hang out, Soap Bar was made for chilling.

St Göran & Draken, Stortorget 22, Gamla Stan.
Tel: 20 59 81
Open: 7am–10pm Monday–Friday; 9am–10pm Saturday;
9am–8pm Sunday.

If you happen to be in the vicinity of Gamla Stan around breakfast-time and have traditional early morning tastes, there are not many better ways to spend an hour on a wintry day than by indulging in a bowl of steaming porridge. All about comfort, it is snug and inviting, decorated in traditional Old Town style; you could while away a good few hours in here among genuine Swedish bits and pieces, which can be few and far between in this area. St Göran & Draken's other big draw is its offer of live music, mostly jazz, which, in the summer, floods out into the old cobbled streets. This is a little way off the James Taylor quartet, but makes for easy listening in a relaxed environment. Drop in on your way to the Royal Palace and pick up one of the music schedules to see what's on. Go in winter and eat something hot. St Göran & Draken's lunchtime soups are as good as their porridge.

Sturehof, Sturegallerien 42, Stureplan 2 Östermalm.
Tel: 440 57 30 www.sturehof.com
Open: 9am–2am Monday–Friday; noon–2am Saturday;
1pm–2am Sunday.

Thanks to its central location in Stureplan next to the exclusive shopping mecca Sture Gallerien, Sturehof has little trouble drawing in the crowds. Another of Stockholm's cafés catering for the hungry, the thirsty and those just up for a party, it boasts a café-cum-restaurant section on the square, its most attractive feature during the summer months and at its best in the middle of the day. Although the menu is predominantly seafood, lunches here

offer plenty of variety, and there is a small oyster bar just through from the restaurant. It is enough simply to sit outside and watch the comings and goings of people at one of the busiest meeting-points in Stockholm.

Sturekatten, Riddargatan 4, Östermalm.
Tel: 611 16 12
Open: 8am–8pm Monday–Friday; 9am–5pm Saturday;
11am–5pm Sunday.

Well known in Stockholm for its traditional cakes and atmosphere, Sturekatten is in some ways reminiscent of the equally old-fashioned Vetekatten. Once you've climbed the winding, rickety staircase you enter a maze of rooms all split up to create different coffee salons. Although slightly kitsch, it feels pretty authentic and any gaudiness is lost in the superiority of the cakes. From the traditional *prinsesstarta* (a cream and marzipan confection) to other, nameless creations, it would be criminal not to try something – but once you have, it's almost impossible not to take home most of what is left on the counter. Popular with locals, the place nevertheless fills up with tourists wanting a piece of 'real' Stockholm. This is one of the few cafés here to feature heavily in guidebooks.

T Bar, Hotel Diplomat, Strandvägen 7.
Tel: 459 68 02
Open: 1pm–midnight daily

Sunday brunch at the T Bar in the lobby of the fashionable Diplomat hotel is an exceedingly chic affair. It's civilized in every sense: this is where elderly parents meet their children, now successful professionals, for baby chat over huge Caesar salads. Chinos, blazers and pearls and immaculate grooming are definitely the order of the day, while the working week sees relatively more relaxed business gatherings. However, T-Bar's café status is drawn less from the weekend events than from its everyday serving of very English afternoon tea. This is the full works: enormous brioche-like scones, home-made jams and marmalades and

as many pots of Earl Grey as you fancy. The simple and comfortable interior contributes to this traditional experience, with mostly neutral colours that grow brighter around the corner where the café becomes a bar. This is great for a few drinks before dinner, especially if you're staying in the hotel; otherwise keep T-Bar for that moment when the tea and scone craving hits.

Tabac, Kornhamnstorg, Gamla Stan.
Tel: 10 15 34
Open: 10am–midnight Sunday–Thursday; 11am–1am
Friday–Saturday.

Just on the edge of Gamla Stan, with Slussen in view over the water, and opening its doors to Södermalm, this is a great spot for a *café au lait* and home-baked brownies for sightseeing sustenance, or tea-time comforts on a rainy day. Inside it is clean and simple. Cream leather benches and stools line the windows, from where you can observe muddled tourists heading into the all-enveloping Old Town. Recently renovated, it now focuses on *tapas* tit-bits and pasta dishes, so there is little point stopping off here for anything more than shelter from a freezing cold day with a steaming mug of coffee or a quick snack. The seating, although perfectly comfortable, is not inspiring and the food good enough for an energy boost for the rest of the afternoon, but no more than that.

Tures, Sturegallerien 10, Grev Turegatan 11, Östermalm.
Tel: 611 02 10
Open: 11.30am–11pm Monday–Friday; noon–8pm
Saturday–Sunday.

After shopping to the point of exhaustion, Tures, situated in one of Östermalm's most easily accessible malls, will come as a welcome break for a quality snack or more substantial lunch. Its image as more café than restaurant results from its location amid Stockholm's most chic fashion stores, even though its service, décor and standard of food deserve restaurant status. As it sits in the middle of a constant stream of shoppers and Östermalm elite, coming here for a low-profile bite to eat is not an option. Instead you should focus on a spot of people-watching with the expectation of being closely observed yourself. Young and cool, this is a meeting-place for the local beauties and, come Friday evenings, a chance for equally glamorous professionals to let their hair down at the very conspicuous bar. No problems finding Tures, since with huge photographs of luscious red lips among other abstract wall hangings, the place appears decadently fascinating, especially when lit up in the evenings. Combine this with its elegant clientele and the popularity of bars such as Grodan just across the way, and you have the ingredients for overall star appeal, whether over a *croque monsieur* at midday or melting calves' liver for an early dinner.

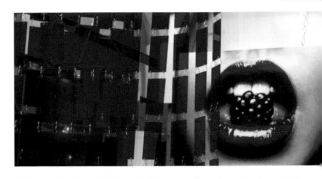

Tvillingarnas, Strandkajsvägen 27, Östermalm/Djurgården.
Tel: 660 37 14
Open: 8am–8pm daily. Closed November–March.

Tvillingarnas, meaning 'the twins', has two major selling-points.
The first is that it is situated on two boats – hence the name.
Tvillingarnas is a floating café, with tables laid along the length of
one of the boats, while the other houses the kitchen. Its second
great advantage is its location. Moored along the architecturally
beautiful Strand, it can be found just next to the Djurgården
Bridge, from where you can see the greenery of the island park.
The lure of brunch on this boat makes a perfect goal for a
morning's walk. The food can take the form of a snack or something more sophisticated and substantial, but either way
Tvillingarnas is undoubtedly a lunch rather than dinner spot. On
sunny days it is unsurprisingly crowded with a local mob. Watch

the passing boats and admire the buildings of the Strand from this ideal viewpoint.

Vetekatten, Kungsgatan 55, Norrmalm.
Tel: 21 84 54
Open: 7.30am–8pm Monday–Friday; 9am–5pm Saturday;
noon–5pm Sunday.

One of Stockholm's most authentic cake shops. Ensure you have a good look around, as you don't want to miss the old-fashioned, doily-filled tea-house, or the adjoining room stuffed with glass cabinets, which in turn are crammed with every kind of chocolate you could wish for. Classic Swedish pastries such as

prinsesstarta – essentially a lot of cream and green marzipan – are sticky and delicious, while the familiar fruit cakes seen in so many cafés are outstanding. Come here for a traditional Scandinavian ambience and mouth-watering delicacies, but don't expect the place to be anything other than rather antiquated and filled with families, younger locals who nostalgically yearn for childhood treats, or tourists who have wandered by and spied something they liked the look of. Trendy this is not.

Zucchero, Bormästargatan 7, Södermalm.
Tel: 644 22 87
Open: 5–11pm Tuesday–Thursday; 5pm–12am Friday;
11am–3pm, 5pm–12am Saturday; 11am–3pm Sunday.

The brightly coloured plastic tablecloths and shabby chairs don't do the Italian food here justice, but the simple décor does fit the down-to-earth atmosphere. It is also very typical of the area, blending in with the bohemian feel of Södermalm's restaurants, which focus less on interior design and more on the mood created by the clientele. As a result the vibe is relaxed and friendly, and the dishes are the staples of home-cooked Italian comfort food. Varieties of pasta and pizza are followed up by gelati and tiramisu, generous portions of food served up in huge white bowls. Zucchero was awarded the Stockholm prize as best café in 2000. Ignore the 1950s theme and enjoy a zesty Italian filled with lots of heart and enthusiasm.

party...

Almost inevitably, bars in Stockholm turn into a place to party after midnight. Although this is true of many capital cities, in terms of aesthetics and people some of the nightclubs here are like few others in Europe. Café Opera and Laroy are great examples, stunning in design and attracting a hip and beautiful crowd.

Sophisticated and cool, a certain breed of Stockholmer really knows how to party in style and go all out to drink, dance and attract attention. But if you're looking for more low-key revelry, Cliff Barnes might be more up your street, with its down-to-earth atmosphere and less determinedly conspicuous players.

Wherever you are, things start late and go on until the early hours. It's traditional in Stockholm either to stay at home or go to a bar until long after midnight before hitting the clubs. This gives you a safe 3- or 4-hour time bracket in which to dance the night away, as most clubs don't throw you out until 4 or 5am.

Of course, you'll have to get in. For those not 'in the know' or regulars at these places, the golden rule is to arrive early. At places such as Café Opera it's sensible to book a table and eat there first, to avoid freezing for hours in a mile-long queue outside. Other spots are less difficult — Kharma shouldn't prove prob-

lematic before midnight and even the recently reopened and painfully trendy Sture Compagniet has a flexible door policy early on. Dress well and appear confident. The clubs want to attract certain looks or specific types, so you need to behave accordingly and look like you deserve to be there. Also take note of varying age restrictions – most clubs adopt a 23 and over policy but if you look the part you'll rarely be asked for ID.

For those who prefer a night of jazz to garage beats, Stockholm is less well equipped than some cities. However, the music clubs it does offer are popular and filled with a genuine buzz. Fasching is the best for jazz, offering everything from funk to acid jazz and keeping the crowd going all night. Mosebacke is a famous Stockholm establishment which has, in the past, featured many of Sweden's most recognized jazz artists as well as a variety of other acts ranging from pop to classical.

Casinos in Stockholm are few and far between. The only vaguely respectable one is Casino Cosmopol, not far from Fasching, where you can gamble within reason – until a couple of years ago Stockholm banned casinos, and those that do now exist are governed by extremely strict laws.

In fact the lack of a gambling scene in Stockholm is a reflection on the city's general innocence, a trait also noticeable in the lack of adult entertainment. There are three strip-clubs to speak of, all of which are pretty undesirable. Kino and Privé are located in the centre of town. They have sex shops in their lobbies and are open from mid-afternoon to whenever business runs out.

Berns Salonger, Berzelii Park 9, Norrmalm.
Tel: 566 322 22 www.berns.se
Open: 5pm–12am Sunday–Monday; 5pm–1am Tuesday–
Wednesday; 5pm–4am Thursday–Saturday.

Berns Salonger is almost as glamorous and elegant as the LE club
beneath, but with a more relaxed door policy. In fact, depending
on your mood, this may be your preferred option, since the
music is less hardcore and the scenery, as with the neighbouring
restaurant, spectacular. High ceilings accommodate palm trees
sheltering black leather sofas, while gaudy neon light bounces off
the huge chandeliers. The room is split in two, the bar taking up
one half and the dance-floor (from 11pm) the other. Next door

is the much smaller 'hip-hop' zone, where the suburban boys'
ghetto-fabulous moves put others to shame. It is hot, frenetic
and sweaty, and the glass doors separating the dance-floor from
the bar soon steam up. Both rooms are incredibly vibrant; inhibi-
tions are broken down and everyone dances freely, away from
the critical eyes of garage devotees downstairs. More relaxed,
more mainstream, but far from boring.

Café Momba, Norrmalmstorg, Norrmalm.
Tel: 678 72 72
Open: 9am–2am Friday–Saturday in summer

As with so many places in Stockholm, Momba takes on the role of café, bar and club. Hosted in a marquee in the middle of a smart square, the club is obviously only open in the summer months. At weekends, the white tent basks in a deep red glow, as thumping R&B basslines pound the night sky. Definitely not part of the 'festival' experience, this marquee is sleek, sexy and chic. The atmosphere is undeniably hot, the dancing electric and the clientele seemingly inexhaustible.

Café Opera, Operahuset, Kungsträdgården, Norrmalm.
Tel: 676 58 07 www.cafeopera.se
Open: 11.30–3am Monday–Saturday; 1pm–3am Sunday

Stunning from every angle, Café Opera offers wall-to-wall beauty in terms of people, drinks and décor. This is where Stockholm's elite meets on a Friday night to be seen beneath the chandeliers. Resurrected by a group of hip 20-somethings who have packed this unashamedly opulent space with their friends and those who want to be their friends, the two individual spaces have distinct roles. The grand dining room houses tables of Prada-clad socialites flirting, drinking and teasing each other, while the art-deco conservatory contains the relatively minute dance-floor and darker bar where the less socially aware gather. There is always a queue at weekends, so either book a table for dinner or be prepared to wait for a while. It's worth it.

Cliff Barnes, Nortullsgatan 45, Vasastan.
Tel: 31 80 70
Open: 11-1am Monday–Friday; 6pm–1am Saturday

Here is a rather decrepit-looking house, with old wooden chairs
surrounding old wooden tables, which sit on an equally ancient
wooden floor. Don't be put off – this is the idea. You'll soon find
yourself completely at home among the general tattiness, friendly
staff and simple drinks, about to witness the evening turning into
a great party. Think classy pub food before 11pm, followed by
uncontrolled madness from then on. Cliff Barnes has three rules:
no rudeness, no dancing on tables and no opening of any windows. As a result, this is a noisy, packed, sweaty affair, where
those in the know travel across town to let their hair down. And

this is done in very local style. Drink too much here before opting for greater exclusivity elsewhere, or stick with a reliably entertaining crowd who really know how to party since, in the middle of Vasastan, it's a bit of trek to get back to the more fashionable parts of town.

Cocktail Club, Grev Turegatan 16, Östermalm.
Tel: 679 61 00
Open: 6pm–3am Thursday–Friday; 10pm–3am Saturday–Sunday.

One of the most striking things about Grodan's basement Cocktail Club is the stark contrast with the elegant gourmet restaurant upstairs. Down here the décor is almost sinful: a red glow engulfs both the main bar and the more intimate underground dens leading off it. It feels altogether more grown up, and the space overflows with those who have left Kharma and other

more fun-loving nightclubs in pursuit of 'serious' house music and less frivolous chat. Nevertheless, as its name suggests, rainbow cocktails flow readily among the otherwise more serious goings-on, and these ensure that, come 2am, no one's too cool not to dance. If, after a couple of hours, this less amiable ambience becomes too much of an effort, moving on won't be a problem. Situated in the middle of the Östermalm hub of bars an alternative atmosphere will be just around the corner.

Daily News Café, Kungsträdgården, Norrmalm.
Tel: 21 56 55
Open: 10pm–4am Wednesday; 10pm–3am Thursday;
10pm–5am Friday; 9pm–5am Saturday.

Less well known than most in this area – the über-chic Café
Opera is a mere 100 metres away – the Daily News Café offers
late-night respite. Come 4am, temperatures of –10°C and an
unwillingness to go home, this is the place for the die-hard club-
ber with an hour of unexpended energy remaining. It's based
over several floors: an unusually light-hearted DJ plays 1970s
disco and Motown classics to an unpretentious crowd on the
ground floor, while hard house and techno are mixed on the
upper levels. The décor and clientele are not exactly stylish, but
Daily News provides a useful alternative to the queues of Café
Opera as well as shelter from the cold night air.

Elverket, Linnégatan 69, Östermalm.
Tel: 661 25 62
Open: 11am–2pm Monday; 11am–1am Tuesday–Sunday.

A great restaurant during the week, which converts at weekends
less to a club than to a general party. Pick your night depending
on your music preference, with funk on Thursdays, country on
Fridays and indie/hard rock during the weekend. You'll find few

tourists here as the more well-known places tend to hog the limelight, especially during the weekends. Here it is more about the music than seeing and being seen. Elverket can provide everything from *tapas*-style food to arty stage performances in their theatre next door, and dancing into the early hours. The theatrical side of things brings in an educated clientele, but the crowd will generally be determined by whatever the place is offering on any given night. If you're feeling soulful, sit on cushlons and listen to blues, or otherwise dance the night away far from the pretensions of other better known clubs.

Kharma, Sturegatan 10, Östermalm.
Tel: 662 04 65
Open: 6–11pm Thursday; 11pm–3am Wednesday–Saturday.

Thursday is Kharma day – that's the general cry from Stockholm's social elite; you will find most of the Östermalm *fashionistas* here. Despite its popularity, you're unlikely to be faced with the prospect of long queues and strict door policies. Kharma's slightly more relaxed attitude might have something to do with the opening of Sture Compagniet next door – it will need to fight to maintain its Thursday night status. Stick to the golden rule of arriving early and you should walk in without having to force your way through a late-night drunken build up. Inside East meets West: Oriental lanterns, wicker baskets and

lacquer chests contrast with an overbearing pink neon bar; the décor sets the mood for the club, although the restaurant offers good Asian nibbles earlier on in an adjoining section. Two dance-floors, bars and DJs should provide enough variety for most, although if you're after an underground beat, then its probably better to look elsewhere. If you prefer to observe rather than take part, however, deep sofas provide relief for sore feet and proper appreciation of a great cosmopolitan atmosphere.

Koket, Sturegatan 4, Östermalm.
Tel: 611 65 79
Open: 11pm–3am Thursday–Saturday

In the basement of Sture Compagniet, Koket (meaning 'kitchen') is far more significant as a club than the restaurant to which its

name refers. The clean and white upstairs, with bottles of Smirnoff lined up on a stripped bar, contrasts dramatically with the sinful red basement. Shadowy figures lip-read through increasingly loud music as the night progresses. Sture Compagniert's reopening seems not to have affected Koket's popularity – when people get bored upstairs, they just wander down to a darker, wickeder scene.

The Lab, Birger Jarlsgatan 20, Östermalm.
Tel: 545 037 02
Open: 5pm-midnight Monday-Wednesday, 5pm-3am weekends.

The Lab, under the same management as Laroy and the Spy Bar, is the most easily accessible of the three clubs. Next door to the Spy Bar, it is the third of this party trio. Essentially just a bar and small lounge, after midnight at weekends it turns into a dance venue with a packed and sweaty dance-floor where the overflow from Laroy and the Spy Bar gyrate to mixed beats. You can hear the noise, drum'n'bass to pop, half-way down Birger Jarlsgatan.

Leave it for a post Laroy experience, as the later it gets the more fun it is.

Laroy, Birger Jarlsgatan 20, Östermalm.
Tel: 545 037 00
Open: 5pm–midnight Monday–Wednesday;
5pm–3am Thursday–Saturday.

Once upon a time Laroy would have been number one on most people's list as THE place to be on a Friday or Saturday, but now the section of Stockholm's beautiful people who champion it has dwindled somewhat. Although the levels of general aesthetic magnificence, both in terms of place and party people, has not declined in the least, the nearby competition, Berns and Café Opera, has ensured that merely a couple of drinks in Laroy will suffice before moving on. Nubile young things are the order of the day here and this may be one reason for Laroy's waning success. You can't move, literally, for the vast quantities of 19-year-olds sporting 'J'adore Dior' T-shirts, and if you're over the age of 23 (21 is the official age of entry), expect to feel past the peak of your youthful prime. Glitz from the luxuriant furnishings on two floors, and a packed dance-floor of designer-clad creatures gyrating to typical chart toppers makes for heaven or hell, depending entirely on who you are and what you expect from a top night out.

LE, Berzelli Park 9, Norrmalm.
Tel: 566 322 22 www.berns.se
Open: 10pm–4am Thursday–Saturday

Converting from conference centre to über-club as the weekend draws nearer, this venue manages its mutation with such aplomb that you'd never guess this could be anything but the ultra cool, drum'n'bass-filled space that presents itself on weekends. Unlike

many of the basement clubs in town, this is much fresher in its look: white fabric streams downs walls, reflecting the pink projected light. Black leather seating is pushed aside to make room for one of the largest dance-floors in Stockholm, for the people who frequent LE are here to dance. The garage and underground sounds are unexpected for somewhere like this, but the enthusiasm for an alternative to Berns' more mainstream club upstairs is palpable. Members-only in theory, the club is sympathetic to early arrivers, although be prepared to use your most persuasive tactics and hippest attire to convince the man at the door of your worthiness. Berns Hotel guests get automatic entry, although this is by no means a sound indication of the type of people you'll find here. Mostly it is those who really love LE and the music it offers who are prepared to beg, borrow or steal to get in. Open till 4 and packed until not a minute before on Friday and Saturday nights.

Metró, Götgatan 93, Södermalm.
Tel: 673 38 00
Open: 5pm–1am Monday–Saturday

Owned by the same management as the newly opened Isole, Metro has a reputation that should ensure the success of the former. It's populated largely by a diverse Södermalm mob, but people from elsewhere in town are more than prepared to travel to this unlikely location for Metro's alternative atmosphere.

Slickly designed in red and black, and creating the illusion of enormity through its several levels, this place can seemingly fit most of Södermalm inside it. Arrive early for guaranteed entry, although south Stockholm's lack of pretentiousness means bouncers are less discriminating about who they let in. If you don't quite hit the 23 age mark, though, dress to impress as they're stricter than some venues about the law.

O Baren, Stureplan 2, Östermalm.
Tel: 440 57 30 www.sturehof.com
Open: 7pm–2am daily

Although many of the best places are located centrally, it is Sturehof, with its restaurant, bar and club, that takes real pride of

place, bang in the middle of Stureplan. O Baren, Sturehof's upstairs space, is the focal point that gathers a fashionable crowd. The benchmark for this comes in the form of DJs and live acts playing anything from bass-heavy hip-hop to hard rock music. Dark and smoky, O Baren has the feel of an old-school jazz club, but with an atmosphere more pretentious than chilled. This is not so much a criticism as a warning: most regulars are deeply involved in their music and, more often than not, media chat. Different levels present great opportunities for people-watching, and here that will rarely get boring. There's no official dance-floor, but the clientele's enthusiasm for music ensures more than just a gentle tapping of feet amid conversation.

Olssons Skor, Oldengatan 41, Vasastan
Tel: 673 38 00 www.storstad.info
Open: 4pm–1am (3am Friday and Saturday). Closed Sunday.

Rather unassuming and named, quite literally, after the 'Olssons Shoes' shop that was here before it, this Vasastan venue may be one of the most hidden yet popular places to party this side of town. When the co-owned Storstad next door became overrun with *fashionistas* wanting to use its well-equipped bar as much as sample its delicacies, the management expanded into the adjacent shoe shop. Now you will find no trace of any cobbling activities; instead, there's a neon sign, a huge aquarium and high

leather-covered bar stools surrounding a double levelled bar.
Tiny, this place crams in more people than must be good for it
on weekends, and with the sound-proofed interior bar, muted
lighting and only a fish tank offering a distorted view of the outside world, you could lose your sense of time and location.
Projections of nameless cities light up walls above red leather
banquettes, perfect on which to sip vanilla vodka before dancing,
independent of a formal dance-floor, to everything from ABBA to
drum'n'bass.

Spy Bar, Birger Jarlsgaten 20, Norrmalm.
Tel: 611 65 00
Open: 10pm–5am. Closed Sunday.

This is possibly Sweden's most famous nightspot, but don't take
that as a guarantee of its overall superiority and impressiveness.
Spy Bar has had to keep up with the very contemporary ideas of
its increasing number of rivals, but in fact it seems that little rein-
vention is needed, since this converted grand apartment continues to attract a large enough combination of suburban clientele
and Swedish holiday-makers to rattle on successfully. The idea
works – high ceilings in decoratively contrasting rooms, gold and
velvet juxtaposed with straight and simple, and great acoustics
for equally alternating styles of music. Despite much hype about
the VIP 'Red Room', with heavy curtains separating it from the

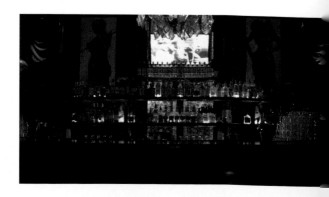

very unshabby 'non-exclusive' sections, waste no time trying to talk your way in here, as the people are no prettier and the drinks double the already extreme prices at the normal bar. You'd have thought, judging by the excessively fastidious bouncers, that getting in to Spy Bar was tantamount to finding the Holy Grail, but don't waste energy fighting for too long, as battles on the doors of other nearby clubs may prove more fruitful and, once inside, more worthwhile too.

Sture Compagniet, Sturegaten 4, Östermalm.
Tel: 611 78 00
Open: 11.30am–1am or 3am Monday–Wednesday;
11.30am–5am Thursday–Saturday.

After a decline in popularity a couple of years ago, Sture Compagniet has now reopened, bigger, better and in theory about to regain its status as the most exclusive club in Stockholm. Whether this is a reality or not, the management have had no qualms in keeping standards high in terms of clientele – dress up, arrive early and exude diva-like confidence to ensure entry. Internally Sture adopts cinematic perfection in the form of three floors of varying décor, atmosphere and music style. A pedantic door policy doesn't prevent an interesting fusion of suburbia, celebrity and socialite cropping up inside. At least for now, the word 'Sture' still conjures up enough of an awe-inspiring image to bring hopefuls from near and far.

Whatever your disposition, you will find something that caters for your preferences, and for the girls this may just mean chatting with friends in the fabulous ladies' loo! Here, we are talking mega-bathroom – a bathroom the likes of which you've probably never seen; it is half the size of one of Sture's huge floors and accommodates enough white leather chairs and floor-to-ceiling mirrors to ensure that idle gossip in here can go on for hours.

MUSIC CLUBS

Fasching Jazzclub, Kungsgaten, 63, Norrmalm.
Tel: 21 62 67 www.fasching.se
Open: 7pm–1am Monday–Thursday; Latino Club 10.30pm–4am Friday, Soul Club midnight–3am Saturday.

You know, as you reach the entrance of Fasching, that this is going to be everything you want a jazz club to be. It's legendary in Stockholm, and appreciation of the music is what it's all about: with jam sessions and concerts six nights a week, the music just keeps on coming. Call before you go to confirm that what you want is what you're going to get, as with everything from funk to Latin to soul jazz, it would be a travesty not to enjoy Fasching as much as you could. The only guarantee is that Fridays produce

salsa and Saturdays soul – a 10-year-old clubbing institution in this case, rather than just a style of music. On these nights in particular, regulars flock in to listen and dance to sounds from the last three decades, which still have everyone on their feet come 4am. Find relief in the form of a crowd who are less style- than music-conscious, and whose true appreciation of jazz and blues cannot fail to get you involved in the genuine mood any day of the week.

Mosebacke, Mosebacke Torg 3, Södermalm.
Tel: 556 098 90 www.mosebacke.se
Open: 4–10pm Monday–Friday; noon–10pm Saturday–Sunday.

Mosebacke is home to some of the finest and most sophisticated musicians in Stockholm. Jazz, pop, rock, salsa and reggae all blend together to create individual combinations of live music. International DJs come and play at weekends, and some enjoy it

so much they return to do sets for free. Friday's funky jazz, soul and hip-hop night; and Saturday's raw fusion of club sounds and Latino music draw in a genuinely attentive crowd. The clientele are slightly older than other clubs but the atmosphere remains fantastic. In summer the outdoor terrace offers a great view of Stockholm and allows you to raise a glass and enjoy the white nights.

Stampen, Stora Nyg 5, Gamla Stan.
Tel: 20 57 93.
Open: 8pm–1am Monday–Thursday; 8pm–2am Friday–Saturday.

This small jazz club is hidden among the picture-perfect streets of Gamla Stan. Its appeal, mainly to tourists, is based on its intimacy, allowing a relationship to form between audience and musicians. The two floors offer different styles of music: downstairs fosters a country and funk vibe while upstairs adheres more to traditional jazz. Its décor is a mix of stereotypical jazz

club and Old Town kitsch. Pots and pans hanging from the ceiling are juxtaposed with the typical photographs and paintings of famous jazz musicians – both domestic and international. Stampen is a great place to pop into for an hour mid-evening to enjoy a chilled-out drink with a couple of friends.

CASINOS

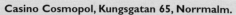

Casino Cosmopol, Kungsgatan 65, Norrmalm.
Tel: 781 88 00
Open: 1pm–5am daily

Although there are other smaller, much less appealing casinos in Stockholm, this is the only one that is even vaguely reminiscent of Las Vegas. The management have gone all-out to add the necessary glitz to draw in a Stockholm clientele who are unfamiliar, owing to past gambling laws, with the joys of blackjack and roulette. The setting is elegantly European; newly restored artwork and shimmering drapes hang from the 18-foot high ceilings. Locals are not so much into their betting as good-old fashioned partying, so you are more likely to find large amateur groups and hopeful tourists there purely for the entertainment factor, or the more serious lone businessmen bored with room service and cable TV. Although the casino is located in a central shopping area, there is no particular reason why you would be walking past of an evening, so it is unlikely that you'll just wander by and have a flutter on impulse. As far as clubs nearby are concerned, Fasching next door is one of the very few venues within walking distance, but after a night of soulful blues the casino will seem more vulgar than entertaining.

ADULT ENTERTAINMENT

The world of adult entertainment is, to say the least, limited in Stockholm. The three main strip-clubs, Kino, Prive and Cabaret School, are similar and have zero class, being seedy in the extreme. Usually empty from opening to closing, since Stockholm locals don't waste their time looking for cheap thrills here but head to Denmark, especially Copenhagen, for weekends of adult fun. If you do find yourself in one of these grim establishments, you can expect the usual pole dancing, very unspecial VIP section and several back rooms where massages etc. are performed. Kino has a sex shop in its lobby, which is about the most notable thing the club has to offer. If you think a quick drink, just to check the places out, is a possibility, think again – no alcohol is sold in any of the clubs and you will instead be placated with a suggested non-alcoholic gin 'essence' and tonic or some such unlikely concoction. All in all, to be avoided at all costs – head elsewhere if you're after the red light scene.

culture...

Stockholm is a simply stunning city. As it was built on a number of small islands, the city's growth and heritage have always been inextricably linked with the sea. While it has a number of first-rate museums and galleries, the biggest draws tend to be connected in some way with the water. The Vasa Museum provides a breathtaking journey into Sweden's past – the eponymous warship is as awesome a relic as you'll see anywhere. The sheer scale of it meant that only the first hundred feet of mast could be included within the museum; the remainder towers above its mausoleum like a beacon on the landscape.

The art museums, the Modern and the National, house impressive collections. Although Stockholm is not exactly renowned for its internationally inspiring galleries the Museum of Modern Art holds some striking pieces by innovative and inventive artists. Innovation is echoed in Sweden's design expertise: intense simplicity, and adherence to form and functionality are the order of the day.

The Nordic Museum, Skansen and the Royal Palace are all testaments to times gone by. They provide varied and fascinating insights into Stockholm's past life. The Palace will not disappoint those who like to spend a Sunday afternoon taking in the delights of a British stately home or paying the perennial summer

visit to see the latest attractions at Buckingham Palace. The Nordic Museum and Skansen, meanwhile, are poles apart – one a practical, living anthropological museum that attracts small children with a menu of education followed by roller-coasters while the Nordic Museum simply offers the education. That said, it is housed in a stunning neo-Gothic building that has become a landmark on the shores of Djurgården.

Which brings us neatly to Djurgården, the island park – or is that the park island? Larger than Hyde Park, Djurgården provides a real slice of the country-side just 10 minutes' walk from the centre. Imagine walking through Hyde Park and coming across a family home with children and dogs spilling out of the doors; and paths that stretch through the wilderness so one can truly escape, go for a jog, gently walk off a near fatal amount of lunch or simply stroll hand-in-hand with the one you love for miles in virtual solitude. Without doubt a rural idyll.

If you feel like a night of culture, where better than the opera? Cheaper than Covent Garden, the Opera House stages an eclectic mix of modern and classic performances. If this seems a little highbrow, or if you are still feeling the effects of last night's vodka, then Stockholm has a plethora of cinemas that show both arty Scandinavian films and the top American blockbusters.

Djurgården

An essential part of the Stockholm experience. Djurgården's treasures include everything from a zoo to the best museum in town. Equally, if you just want to walk off lunch, there are countless routes you can take which will satisfy both the very energetic and the less enthusiastic rambler. Earn yourself a sticky cake at Rosendals Tradgard (see page 140) after a lengthy stroll, or take time out to wander around the delights of Skansen, the open-air museum (see below).

Moderna Museet, Skeppsholmen.
Tel: 519 552 00 www.modernamuseet.se
Open: 10am–8pm Tuesday–Thursday; 10am–6pm Friday–Sunday.

Over the last 50 years the Museum of Modern Art, voted Museum of the Year, has built up an impressive collection of works that includes pieces by Picasso, Matisse, Miró, Duchamp and Rauschenberg. The permanent collections of art and photography are supplemented by further exhibitions, primarily concentrating on Nordic artists but also housing important displays of prominent 20th-century figures. The avant-garde building, originally built in 1998, and designed by Spanish architect Rafael

Moneo, is a fitting home for such a magnificent modern collection. Located on an island, just along from the Grand Hotel, the Museet is in a beautiful setting, looking over the water and across to the façade of the Grand and, just beyond, Stockholm's Operahuset.

National Museum, Sodra Blasieholmen.
Tel: 519 543 00 www.nationalmuseum.se
Open: 11am–8pm Tuesday, Thursday (5pm June–August);
11am–5pm Wednesday, Friday–Sunday.

The largest art museum in Sweden deserves the attention of the most avid and exacting art critic. The building itself is reminiscent

of Florentine and Venetian Renaissance architecture, and houses Scandinavian paintings, sculptures and ornaments, some of which date back to the 16tth century. During the summer guided tours in English are available, but it's possibly more fun to work your way through the rooms on your own, picking and choosing what to see. The museum's collection comprises works of the great Old Masters (Rembrandt, Goya and Rubens), Impressionists and Post-Impressionists (Renoir, Degas and Gauguin) and 18th- and 19th-century Swedish painters (Larsson, Josephson and Zorn). Alongside these, the National has a section dedicated to applied art and modern design, as well as exhibitions that change monthly. If you are lucky enough to be staying at The Grand, the National Museum is almost on your doorstep. Scandinavian arts can be viewed over a cup of coffee in Atrium, the museum's first class café.

Nordiska Museet, Djurgårdsvagen 6–16.
Tel: 519 560 00 www.nordiskamuseet.se
Open: 10am–4pm daily (5pm July–August).
Closed Monday throughout September to June.

If you're after cultural history in an awe-inspiring building, Nordiska Museet is the place for you. Since it's located next to the Vasa Museum, you can cover both these treasures in a morning. Nordiska is the creation of Arthur Hazelius, also responsible for Skansen, and its massive building houses everything from life-

size dolls, scarily bringing Coppelia to mind, to exhibitions dedicated to Swedish traditions. Charting the advancements and achievements of the Nordic people, the museum is mesmerizing, but if you try to see the collection in any logical order, you'll be there all day, so spend some time when you arrive picking out the exhibits that most interest you.

The Royal Palace, Gamla Stan.
Tel: 402 61 30 www.royalcourt.se
Open: 10am–4pm daily, mid-May–August; 12–3pm,
Tuesday–Sunday, September–mid-May.

Towering over the old winding streets of Gamla Stan, the yellow façade of the Royal Palace can be seen from most points in Stockholm. The Royal Family no longer live here, despite it

remaining their official residence, but it still seems satisfactorily regal and there are enough museums and apartments open to the public to make it worth a visit. The Royal Apartments are especially opulent, while the Museum Tre Kronor next door tells the story of the palace through the decades. Don't go to too many lengths to experience every part, since there are enough exhibits and beautiful rooms to keep you going for most of a day. Pick the most appealing, probably the Apartments, and get a feel for the place from this.

Saluhallen, Östermalmstorg, Östermalm.

Saluhallen is the large covered fresh produce market, home to the Lisa Elmqvist and Gerda's restaurants (see pages 83 and 75). Inside you can buy anything from the richest chocolate cake to fish caught that morning. Ideally located in one of Östermalm's most appealing market squares, Saluhallen is a foodie's dream: you'll take in your first breath of air and sigh contentedly as you enter. This is the haunt of Stockholm's social elite, from the young hotshots who don't have time to cook to the older wives who have pretended for years that Saluhallen's exquisite ready-made meals are their own inventions. Well worth a visit just to soak up the atmosphere, smells and, inevitably, tastes.

Sightseeing Boats, Strömkajen, Norrmalm.
Tel: 587 140 20 www.stockholmsightseeing.com

Stockholm is a city built on multiple islands at the edge of an archipelago, so water is a dominant feature. It would be a crime to come here and not to head out in a boat for a morning or afternoon to witness the beauty of the archipelago or take a trip around the islands. This can be done on an organized tour (details above) or by simply catching the ferries that run between the islands. The locals are very proud of this side of

their city, and will encourage you to take a trip out, especially in the summer months.

Skansen, Djurgården.
Tel: 442 80 00 www.skansen.se
Open: 10am–4pm (October–April), 5pm (September),
8pm (May), 10pm (June–August).

This is Stockholm's number-one attraction and rightly so, appealing to everyone from the ages of 3 to 93. With more than a million visitors every year it combines an open-air museum with an amusement park and zoo, and stretches for miles. It is almost worth coming to Stockholm for this alone, for between wander-

ing around the crocodile houses and taking a heart-stopping roller-coaster ride, there is something for everyone. It's popular with locals as well as with tourists, and is in fact one of the few local attractions that draws more Swedish visitors than curious holiday-makers.

Vasamuséet, Djurgården.
Tel: 519 548 00 www.vasamuseet.se
Open: 10am–5pm daily (8pm Wednesday).

The Vasa is a sight to behold. Just over the bridge into Djurgården, you'd have to be feeling really lazy not to bother with this museum. The huge warship *Vasa* sank in Stockholm waters in 1628. Discovered in the 1950s, the ship, now refurbished, is displayed here, along with intricate models illustrating her rescue and more gruesome films detailing the perils of life on board. Endlessly entertaining, you could easily lose yourself here for an entire morning. Massively popular, you'll find yourself among hordes of camera-clutching visitors, but enthusiasm for this sight is irresistible. If you only want to visit one museum on your trip, this should be it.

OPERA

Opera House, Strömgatan, Norrmalm.
Tel: 24 82 40 www.operan.se

The Opera House is set just across the water from the Royal Palace and holds an impressive conglomerate of bars, restaurants and nightclubs within the same building. Internally, the grand and sumptuous architecture lends weight to the fantastic programme. Modern and classic operas written by the great composers as well as by contemporary Swedes take pride of place. Ballets and operas are performed here almost every night of the week, with ticket prices rarely exceeding 500kr.

CINEMA

No problem finding cinemas in Stockholm, from the huge complexes with cafés and bars to the smaller venues showing more alternative films. Both usually show films in English with Swedish subtitles, although it's worth checking. Films come out at approximately the same time as in other major European cities, although you might have to wait a little longer for those outside the American blockbuster league. Two of the most central cinemas showing mainstream films in English are the Astoria and Rigoletto.

Astoria, Nybrogatan 15, Östermalm.
Tel: 660 00 25 www.sandrews.se

Built in 1928, this is one of the few single-screen cinemas remaining in Stockholm. The Astoria plays mainly American blockbusters within a classic 1920s red-plush interior.

Rigoletto, Kungsgatan 18, Norrmalm.
Tel: 26 00 00 www.sf.se

Seven screens show everything from the newest blockbuster art movies.

TICKETS

For the most sophisticated theatres, concerts and sport events, tickets can be booked by phone at Biljett Direkt and, in person or by phone, at Box Office. The latter is conveniently located under Café Momba on Normalmstorg. There is rarely much of a queue and you'll often find last-minute tickets for the most popular shows.

Biljett Direkt
Tel: 077 170 70 70 www.tcnet.se

Box Office, Normalmstorg, Norrmalm.
Tel: 10 88 00 www.boxoffice.se

shop...

Shopping in Stockholm is a joy, and the shops themselves are simple, efficient and stylish. In recent years Scandinavia, and Sweden in particular, has become renowned for its design. The clean wooden lines, glass and functionality that have come to characterize Scandinavian style are inevitably picked up in many of the bars, restaurants and hotels in town. Today, there are many small specialist design shops dotted around town that sell cutting-edge furniture to kit out the apartments of the style-conscious locals.

The different parts of town offer a variety of shopping experiences. Östermalm, the Chelsea or Knightsbridge of Stockholm, specializes in fashion boutiques and exclusive design shops that represent most of the major domestic and international labels. The residents of Östermalm are highly fashion-conscious and need to look good to strut their stuff in the many super-chic and hip bars that epitomize the area.

Norrmalm, just to the west of Östermalm, is home to the financial and business district as well as some excellent shops. The department stores Åhléns, NK and PK Huset have proved enormously popular. NK is Stockholm's equivalent of Selfridges and its many concessions sell top-of-the range domestic and interna-

tional fashion. Some good international chain stores such as Zara and H&M can be found in Hamngatan.

For more alternative and bohemian boutiques set in small independent shops and truly reflecting the street fashion of Stockholm, go to Södermalm. Although there are no distinct areas where the shops are congregated, it is well worth strolling down Götgatan or Hornsgatan and popping inside the odd boutique.

You won't find too many tourists around here.

The Old Town, Gamla Stan – the centre of Stockholm's tourist trade – is packed with boutiques selling traditional and 'authentic' products. Swedish glass and crystal is renowned throughout Europe, so you'll find quite a lot in these little souvenir shops, along with plenty of little wooden trinkets and the ubiquitous models of Stockholm's monuments. Arts, crafts and antiques can be found everywhere – it is best just to wander the narrow streets, gently browsing through all the small shops have to offer.

If you can't visit Sweden without a trip to IKEA, do it in Stockholm. The city has the world's largest IKEA, and that's saying something.

Åhléns, Klarabergsgatan 50, Norrmalm.

Mid-range, and in a less exclusive part of town, this department store is nevertheless very central. Clothes range from own brand to designer, and there are also cosmetics, glass and a good music department. Bear in mind the fact that you can have a facial on the top floor in the Åhléns Day Spa.

Biblioteksgatan, Östermalm.

Just off Stureplan, and with designers all around, Biblioteksgatan accommodates a similar collection to Birger Jarlsgatan, next to it, and includes the following boutiques:

Don & Donna Interesting, slightly alternative footwear for the young, chic, up-and-coming Östermalm inhabitant.

Emporio Armani What more is there to say? Classic favourites at every turn.

Face Stockholm Another branch of this chain. Simple packaging enhances its straight-up approach to looking good.

Rizzo Designer heels for women and classics for men in the form of Paul Smith, Boss and own-label shoes.

Birger Jarlsgatan, Östermalm.

All the usual suspects line this elite street, which also features high-class restaurants such as Riche, and the delights of the waterfront Strand at one end. Stureplan can be found about halfway down.

Cerruti Scent and fashion from this renowned store.

Gucci Classic Italian fashion and accessories. For certain people, it never goes out of style.

Hugo Boss The thinking man's fashion house: practical, stylish and omnipresent across continental Europe.

Louis Vuitton Distinctive designer luggage, high French fashion and authors of up-market travel guides.

Max Mara Italian fashion, make-up and sunglasses, all designed to make a woman look her most glamorous.

Miss Sixty Young fashion epitomized by denim and alternative design.

Norrgavel Offering Scandinavian furniture with a Japanese minimalist twist, this is typical of the type of store on this street, but Norrgavel tempts you in with its home accessories and knick-knacks.

Orrefors & Kosta Boda With its selection of Sweden's famous glass and crystal, it's not surprising that this shop is expensive, but pop in anyway to admire some traditional Scandinavian glass-work.

Rönnells Antikvariat Sells expensive and rare antiquarian books.

Versace We're sure that if Elton John lived in Stockholm it would be somewhere near here.

Gallerian, Hamngatan 37, Norrmalm.

The first of Stockholm's many malls to open, Gallerian is now less popular than some of the chic and ultra-modern department stores that have sprung up around it. Come here for more everyday needs, and perhaps pick up a few items of clothing (which is noticeably cheaper here). It seems to be packed with good-quality high-street chains.

Carphone Warehouse Just in case. This is the most central branch for dealing with those minor problems.

Pocketshop With hundreds of contemporary English titles, Pocketshop is on a par with Stockholm's more talked-about bookshops (such as Hedengrens).

Twilit Good for underwear and nightwear within a reasonable price bracket.

Vero Moda One of Stockholm's most ubiquitous high-street women's fashion stores.

● **Hamngatan, Norrmalm.**

Shops galore line this very main street, although most of the gems are found within the two main department stores/malls of NK and PK Huset. Other nearby outlets include:

H&M Huge and perfect for those in search of a cheap T-shirt or jersey. The choice is endless.

Polarn o Pyret Striped designs and comfy fabrics for children and adults alike. Casual wear, in every sense of the phrase.

Sverigebokhandelm Well-stocked bookshop with plenty of English titles.

Vero Moda H&M's main Swedish competitor, offering similar sorts of garments.

Zara Just opened, and Stockholm's fashion-conscious men and women have fallen upon this ever more internationally popular high-street store.

187

Hötorget, Norrmalm.

This is the closest that Stockholm gets to an outdoor market. During the week the stalls sell fresh fruit and flowers, while on Sundays these are replaced by antiques, books and general bric-à-brac. Overshadowed by the PUB department store and the Concert Hall, it is a good place to visit on a warm summer's day.

NK, Hamngatan 18–20, Norrmalm.

Stockholm's designer haven, packed to overflowing with expensive boutiques. If you're willing to flex the plastic, then this is the place to come – the city's answer to Selfridges or Harvey

Nichols. Selling everything you'd expect, from cosmetics and accessories to Versace dresses, the store itself is a pleasure to wander round. It is elegantly designed, with an atrium that looks up from the basement to all the departments. The top floor houses one of the best English bookshops in town, while Café Entre downstairs provides light relief from the heavy expenditure. Only the knowledge that NK was the scene of the tragic stabbing of Swedish Foreign Minister, Anna Lindh, in autumn 2003 could mar your enjoyment of the place.

PK Huset, Hamngatan, Norrmalm.

Slightly down-market in comparison to its neighbour, NK, PK Huset is still pricey but more immediately reminiscent of high-street establishments. Some of the most popular Swedish boutiques are found here, along with the ubiquitous H&M. Prime pickings in this mall include:

Champagne Mid-range to designer women's clothes.
Face Stockholm You'll find bigger and better branches of this clean cosmetic chain elsewhere in Stockholm, but this one provides the essentials. Make-up hoarders could spend a while here.

PUB, Drottninggatan 53, Norrmalm.

If you get to Hotorget, you might find yourself more interested in the outside market on the square than in this relatively unexciting but enormous store. Although shopping, for clothes in particular, might be better reserved for NK or some of the little boutiques in malls elsewhere, it should not be forgotten that PUB can probably be relied upon for any minor needs.

Saluhallen, Östermalmstorg, Östermalm.

Located just off Östermalmstorg, this is one of Stockholm's gems. A covered food hall which abounds with the most

tempting-looking fresh produce – meat, fish, vegetables and many more little luxuries, which form the basis for many a sophisticated dinner party. The market houses two delightful restaurants, Lisa Elmqvist and Gerda's (see pages 83 and 75), which make ideal lunch spots; you just know the food is going to be fresh.

Sturegallerien, Stureplan, Östermalm.

If you're staying anywhere around Stureplan, you're likely to find yourself here more than anywhere, shopping-wise. Easy to wander round for an hour or so, it houses Hedengrens, a fantastic bookshop, and clothes and make-up boutiques for the well-heeled Östermalm crowd. It has the added bonus of two very popular restaurants – Tures and Sturehof (see pages 146 and 143) – both great for an early evening drink or quick bite to eat mid-spending. Don't forget the inconspicuous Sturebadet (see page 201), which is, without doubt, the most luxurious Stockholm day spa for a traditional Swedish massage.

Ajas – Sensual lingerie to make the weekend go with a bang.
Bjorn Borg – Sportswear and streetwear from this iconic Swedish sporting legend.
Hedengrans – An excellent bookshop supplying a range of English language books and travel guides.
The Shirt Factory – A range of smart gentlemen's and ladies shirts.

play...

Stockholm offers a variety of different opportunities for both the adventurously minded and those intent on sedate luxury. Given the obvious differences between the long, bright and warm summer days and the sub-zero, snowy and short winter days the activities on offer do tend to be seasonal. The Swedish are a naturally active race and at any given opportunity like to indulge in a little exercise, whether it be cross-country skiing or a short, sharp walk through the countryside.

During the summer months the long days are a joy; after all, it doesn't get dark until past midnight, and even then it's not really dark. Long, leisurely boat trips, evening tennis games and a relaxing round of golf are the order of the day, making the most of the warm sunshine.

In winter you can skate across some of the frozen lakes, head north out of Stockholm for some serious skiing or, if you have the taste for something more confrontational, try a game of ice hockey. Ice hockey is almost a national sport (football just pips it to the post), and is loved and watched by millions. Stockholm has three main teams which compete against each other in hard-

fought derbies. If you have never been to an ice-hockey game before it's well worth it — it's fast, furious and a lot of fun.

If you prefer something less active, or find the whole idea of sport abhorrent, then why not kick back, relax and let yourself be pampered in some of the finest spas in the country? The Yasuragi, just outside Stockholm, focuses on well-being and healthy living, and offers healing treatments and sheer tranquillity, Japanese-style. If you find its emphasis on well-being and healthy living a bit too much, head to Sturebadet, in the centre of town, to preen yourself before embarking on some social conquest.

With so much on offer, there's no excuse for a moment's boredom.

BALLOONING

Throughout the day and for much of the early evening, hot-air balloons, brightly coloured and shimmering, float through the sky above Stockholm. There can be few cities where this activity is so prevalent, and several companies can arrange breathtaking trips. These can also be booked through the Stockholm Information Service (see page 206).

City Ballong, Gästrikegatan 8.
Tel: 33 64 64 www.cityballong.se

Including a champagne-fuelled picnic, this whole experience lasts about 4 hours and is expensive, as you would expect. Prices vary so call to discover the current rates.

BOATING

Unsurprisingly, given the quantities of water flowing in and around this city, boating activities of one sort or another are readily available. These include everything from a sightseeing trip out to the archipelago (see page 176) to a pedalo ride, with canoeing and more serious sailing among the many possibilities too.

Blue Water Cruising Club
Tel: 717 68 00 www.bluewatercruisingclub.com

If you fancy a nautical adventure on a grander scale, you can sail without a skipper for reasonable prices out into the Stockholm archipelago. This club offers smaller boats for hire at a reasonable price, and it also arranges organized tours.

Djurgårdsbrons Sjocafe, Galärvarvsvägen 2, Djurgården.
Tel: 660 57 57

As well as cycles, there are also boats available here, but they tend to be kayaks and canoes rather than anything larger.

**Tvillingarnas, Strandkajsvägen 27,
Östermalm/Djurgården.**
Tel: 660 37 14
Open: 8am–8pm daily, April–October.

This floating waterfront café (see page 147) doubles as a rental
agency for everything from little sailing vessels to motorboats.

BOWLING

Despite Stockholm's rather dubious liking for 'disco bowling', the
original version can be found in centres around the city. You'll be
unlikely to escape without the obligatory loud music and neon
lights, but full-on disco performance can be avoided.

Södra Bowlinghallen, Hornsgatan 54, Södermalm.
Tel: 642 25 00 www.bowlinghallen.com
Open: noon–midnight daily in winter; 4pm–10pm daily in summer.
About 200kr per lane, per hour.

Svea Bowlinghall, Sveavägen 118, Vasastan.
Tel: 441 85 50 www.sveabowlinghall.se

More expensive, with rates of approximately 350kr per lane for
an hour. This bowling hall features a café with sophisticated
Italian nibbles and a generally suave atmosphere.

CYCLING

Stockholm's size, beauty and numerous parks mean that cycling
is a great way to see the sights and get a real feel for the city.
There are plenty of cycle paths, especially in the very central
Djurgården, and bicycles can be hired easily at reasonable prices.

Cykel och Mopeduthyrningen, Kajplats 24 Strandvägen, Östermalm.
Tel: 660 79 59

Roller-blades and mopeds are offered here as well as your traditional bike.

Djurgårdsbrons Sjöcafé, Galärvarvsvägen 2, Djurgården.
Tel: 660 57 57

Next to Skepp & Hoj.

Skepp & Hoj, Djurgårdsbron, Djurgården.
Tel: 660 57 57

Located near the Djurgården Bridge, this is a perfect starting-point for a ride around Stockholm's most central park. Bikes can be rented for about 250kr a day.

FOOTBALL

Football is the biggest spectator sport in the country, and fans have been rewarded by Sweden's constant appearance at European and World cups. However, Stockholm's three main teams, Hammarby, Djurgården and AIK (the most well-known), have not had much success in European club football in recent years. Stockholm has several major stadiums, and there are many matches to choose from, although – as you might expect – Swedish domestic football takes a prolonged break through the winter months but continues through August and September. Hence, many of its top-name stars play in other European leagues.

AIK, Råsunda Fotbollstadion, Solnavägen 51, Solna.
www.aik.se

With a capacity of 37,000, Råsunda is one of the largest stadiums in the country. Home to AIK, it hosts occasional UEFA cup ties.

Hammarby, Söderstadion, Arenavägen.
Tel: 725 12 43 www.hammarbyfotboll.se

Far smaller, this stadium is on a par with some of the UK's Third Division clubs, holding a mere 11,100. However, Hammarby compete in the A League, where they put up a good fight against the likes of Malmö and Göteborg.

For tickets to any of the games, contact the clubs direct, or use a local ticket agency:

Biljett Direkt
Tel: 077 170 70 70 www.biljett.se

One of the biggest ticket brokers in Stockholm.

Box Office, Norrmalmstorg, Norrmalm.
Tel: 10 88 00 www.boxoffice.se

You'll need to visit this shop personally to pick up your tickets, but it's centrally located, just underneath Café Momba.

Globen, Arenavägen, Johaneshov
Tel: 600 34 00; Box Office: 077 131 00 00 www.globen.se

For tickets at this slightly futuristic venue, contact Globen directly.

GOLF

With Swedish golfers Fredrik Jacobson and Annika Sorenstam making a huge impact on the golfing world, the sport is inevitably acquiring an intense following. There are at least 50 golf courses within easy reach of Stockholm's city centre, some more immediately accessible than others. For reliable listings of golf clubs with all the info, email: info@stockholmsgf.golf.se before you leave, or alternatively book yourself in at one of the following:

Djursholms Golfklubb, Hagbardsvägen 1, 182 63 Djursholm.
Tel: 544 96 451 www.dgk.nu

Beautifully set and the closest to the city centre, it has green fees starting at 350kr.

Kungsangen Golf Club, Box 133, 196 21 Kungsangen.
Tel: 584 507 30 www.etc-sthlm.se

This club hosted the 2002 Scandinavian Masters and is a 'serious' course built for equally serious golfers.

Wermdö, Torpa, 139 40 Värmdö.
Tel: 574 607 20 www.wgcc.nu

Within half an hour of the city you hit Wermdö's rolling golf course. Worth the taxi ride there, this boasts the benefits of the countryside just outside Stockholm.

ICE HOCKEY

Swedish fans support their ice hockey teams with gusto during the winter, so much so, in fact, that as a spectator sport it's nearly as popular as football. And, as with football, the major teams are Hammarby, AIK and Djurgården. You can watch these frenetic matches, particularly riotous when it's a derby, at some of the same rinks on which you can skate. The stadiums that stage ice-hockey matches are similar, and everyone tends to play at the Globe Arena (www.globen.se). For tickets and info contact one of the stadiums or individual team websites.

AIK, Globen, Arenavägen, Johaneshov.
Tel: 735 96 00 www.aik.se

AIK play at the Globe Arena, a futuristic rink that can hold up to 13,850 spectators. Although AIK had been league champions since 1984, they have now been relegated from the Premier

Division and are trying to regain their rightful position among the top-flight. It's worth going along to experience the sheer exhilaration and hectic pace of the game.

Djurgården, Globen, Arenavägen, Johaneshov.
Tel: 556 108 00 www.skategate.com

Djurgården also regularly play at the Globe Arena, but unlike AIK they have been more successful in recent times. They won the championship in both 2000 and 2001 and are currently looking to re-establish themselves at the top of the pack.

Hammarby, Globen, Arenavägen, Johaneshov.
Tel: 462 88 25 www.hammarby-if.se

Also playing at the Globe Arena, Hammarby are in the SuperAllsvenskan, the same division as AIK and, as you can imagine, this generates some fierce derby displays.

ICE SKATING

Although most fun in the dead of winter when Stockholm becomes an animated Christmas card, skating can be enjoyed almost any time, since Stockholm inhabitants are so keen on ice hockey that they have enough indoor rinks for the public to use at certain times of day. During the winter it is possible to take prolonged skating trips around the frozen waters of the archipelago, skating from island to island: www.sssk.se explains it all. Skating on the frozen lakes is always a slightly risky business, but for those who prefer the outdoor experience you'll get the authentic feel gliding round one of the following:

Kungsträdgården, Östermalm.
Tel: 789 2490

This is most fun at night when you skate under floodlights. Skate hire is available for 30kr. Call the Swedish tourist office for further details.

Medborgplatsen, Södermalm.
Tel: 789 24 90

Outdoors and tiny, this is mostly full of families and amateur skaters, as there isn't much room for the more adventurous. Skates are very reasonably priced.

Zinkensdamms Idrottplats, Ringvägen 12–14, Södermalm.
Tel: 668 93 31

You'll find games going on here most of the day, which are fun to watch and, if you're feeling brave, you can even take part in a minor way. Otherwise, skate at your own level elsewhere in this huge centre. It's open all year and the admission is free.

KARTING

Go-karting is increasing slowly in popularity, and as yet there really isn't a lot of choice. The best track can be found at:

Racetown, Blekholmsgatan 2, Norrmalm.
Tel: 590 701 70 www.racetown.se

100kr for 7 minutes on the track.

SKIING

If you're a serious skier then you'll have to venture a way out of the city for anything resembling an Alpine slope. However, for a day's amusement, beginning in some cases with a long, early morning bus ride, decent snow at the right time of year isn't a million miles away. Reliable information is available at www.skiinfo.se.

Flottsbro, TomtbergaHuge Fastigheter AB, 141 22 Huddinge.
Tel: 535 327 00 www.flottsbro.com

Located 40km south of the city and intended for the unambitious skier, since the runs are fairly tame. Don't make this more than a day trip.

Kungsberget
Tel: 0290 622 10 www.kungsberget.se

Great for the avid snowboarder, this resort features an impressive half-pipe. To get here you should arrive in Stockholm before the weekend, since the bus leaves at 7am on Saturdays and Sundays to give you time for about 6 hours of snow action.

SPAS

Sturebadet AB, Sturegallerian 36, Östermalm.
Tel: 545 015 00 www.sturebadet.se
Open: 6.30am–10pm Monday–Friday; 9am–7pm Saturday–Sunday.

This is Stockholm's most celebrated spa. With a restaurant so good that it even attracts those not interested in the facilities, and a list of treatments that never ends, it is a luxurious experience from start to finish. It's also perfect for the flying visitor, since you needn't be a member to book a same day appointment here. Drop in for a traditional Swedish massage and relax in a Moroccan-inspired setting – the pool area is decorated with light-blue tiles and is the focal point of the spa. Looking down on this, a well-equipped gym circles the second floor balcony, bisected by the health-conscious restaurant (and if you find that description off-putting, don't worry – the food is delicious). Your list of treatments includes everything from a pedicure to an aromatherapy facial, but the changing rooms are almost the best bit – their musky smelling wood and softly lit saunas will heat you up and chill you out.

Yasuragi, Hasseludden, Hamndalsvägen 6, Saltsjö-Boo.
Tel: 747 61 00 www.hasseludden.com

Functioning as a hotel and conference centre as well as spa, it is hard to know whether to visit Yasuragi for a day or week. As your taxi pulls up to this countryside retreat 15 minutes outside the city centre, don't be disheartened by an uninspiring exterior. Inside, the décor adheres faithfully to its Japanese theme, from the *teppanyaki* restaurant to minimalist bedrooms, with rattan mats on spacious, uncluttered floors and futons to complete the simple mood. It is worth spending a weekend here to reap the full benefits of the Yasuragi health principles, but if a day is all you can spare, you'll still get something special out of it. The food, although intended to be healthy, is so delicious you won't be able to stop eating, which may slightly defeat your original purpose. Treatments, on the other hand, are definitely more Spartan than that of Sturebadet, for example. Staff want you to feel cleansed and detoxed by the end rather than more beautiful. The focus is on, as they put it, inner harmony, but you'll feel pretty good all over by the time you leave. If you have time try one of the numerous yoga or meditation lessons, which will leave you calm and ready to face the outside world.

Skepparholmen, Franckes väg, S-132 39 Saltsjö-Boo.
Tel: 747 65 00 www.skepparholmen.se

Skepparholmen has earned its name through its fantastic spa, although, within 15 minutes of Stockholm's hustle and bustle, it's a valuable countryside retreat even if the spa doesn't interest you. The spa, however, is designed more carefully than the hotel itself; it focuses on cleanliness and comfort, and as you enter the blue and white seating area establishes a pure mood. Pad around in towelling flip-flops and robe for a day or weekend and retire to the spectacular views from your room at the end of the day. Facilities include a swimming pool and gym, but the real features are the treatments and, above all, the massages, which make you so relaxed you never want to leave.

TENNIS

Outdoor tennis courts are available for much of the year, and there are also indoor courts for those keen to play all year round. Book a court in one of the city's most scenic parks or green spaces during the warmer summer months, and an enjoyable game is guaranteed.

Haga Tennis, Hagaparken, Hagalund.
Tel: 33 70 77

Have lunch in the cosy Haga Forum restaurant (**see page 80**) after exertions on these courts, set among charming scenery in the middle of the park. Courts are approximately 100kr an hour.

Kungliga Tennishallen, Lidingövägen 75, Hjorthagen.
Tel: 459 15 00 www.kungl.tennishallen.com

Renowned for hosting the Stockholm Open ATP tournament every year, this is a more expensive place to play. A court for an hour will set you back about 250kr.

Tennisstadion, Fiskartorpsvägen 20.
Tel: 215 454
Open: 7am–11pm Monday–Friday; 8am–9pm Saturday; 8am–10pm Sunday.

Indoor as well as outside courts make this great for year-round enthusiasts. Rackets and balls cost extra to hire on top of the hourly 170kr charge for a court.

WALKING AND HIKING

Clean air, fantastic scenery and the greenery within and around Stockholm's large parks make walking a very pleasurable part of everyday life. For more robust walks, the city and its immediate surrounding areas are limited, so you'll need to investigate hiking trips further north. However, a hearty and pretty lengthy walk is well within the realms of possibility, and there is plenty of choice.

Djurgården

The most obvious and easily accessible space in which to have a reasonably hearty stroll. Don't forget to stop half-way for something sugary at Rosendals Trädgård (see page 140).

info...

DANGERS

Stockholm feels and is very safe. It is not uncommon for locals to leave their cars unlocked when popping into a shop, and anything more serious than burglary is rarely heard of. Watch your bags if traveling on the Tunnelbana, but compared with the problems with pickpockets elsewhere in Europe, Stockholm is not on the map.

MONEY

At the time of writing, the Swedish kroner has a rough exchange rate as follows: £1 = 13kr; Euro1 = 9kr; US$1 = 7kr. It's far easier to get money from cashpoints and banks than it is to take travellers' cheques or money to exchange.

PUBLIC TRANSPORT

Stockholm's tube system, the Tunnelbana, is one of the easiest to use in the world. Tickets to most destinations cost 20kr, directions are clear and the English-speaking staff very helpful. This applies to buses, too, which operate until about midnight daily, when night buses take over.

Never underestimate the usefulness of boats in Stockholm: they are, if you want to travel from one side of the city to the other, often the easiest way to go. The tourist offices have full ferry timetables, as well as information on boat trips out to the archipelago.

QUEUING

Queuing for almost anything in Stockholm involves taking a ticket from a machine and waiting for your number to be called. If you don't take the ticket, your chances of ever being served are minimal.

STOCKHOLM CARD

If you intend to do a lot of sightseeing, save money by buying a Stockholm Card on arrival. This provides free admission to many of Stockholm's museums as well as a host of other attractions, free travel on the Tunnelbana and on many of the sightseeing boats. For more information, call one of the Swedish tourist offices.

Stockholm Information Service, Sverigehuset, Hamngatan 27, Norrmalm.
Tel: 789 24 90 www.stockholmtown.se

Hotellcentralen, Concourse, Central Station, Vasagatan, Norrmalm.
Tel: 789 24 56

TAXIS

The taxi system in Stockholm is rather baffling. Standing on a street corner and trying to hail a cab results in about a 1 in 5 success rate. You are much better advised to get your hotel to call one. If you are staying in one of the bigger places, they are likely to be lined up outside. Fares here must be some of the most expensive in Europe. The meter jumps up at an alarming rate and to get from one side of this small city to the other can cost anything up to about 195–260kr. There is little getting away from it – if you choose this extravagant form of transport, prepare yourself for hefty prices.

Taxi Stockholm – tel: 15 00 00
Taxi Kurir – tel: 30 00 00

TELEPHONES

All the telephone numbers in this book are given without the Stockholm prefix of 08. The international Swedish code is +46. If you are going to be here for a long time and intend to make regular local calls, it is worth buying a Swedish pay-as-you-go SIM.

TIPPING

Tips of 5–10% are expected. As the staff in restaurants are generally among the most helpful around, you may be inclined to leave more. Taxi drivers expect the fare to be rounded up, but no more than this.

index

index